NICOLA PATTERNS

presents

LITTLE DOLLS' CLOTHES

A Collection of Sewing Patterns
for eight complete outfits

To fit all-bisque dolls
13cm to 22cm in height

Joan Nerini

TAFFETA PUBLICATIONS

DEDICATION

To Nicola, my granddaughter.

Text and Patterns   Joan Nerini   .   Copyright 1995
Book/Photo Design   Ferini Designs, Lowestoft, Suffolk.
Photography   Paul Hobbs, Lowestoft, Suffolk.

First edition printed in Great Britain 1995
by Asgard Printing Services, Lowestoft, Suffolk
for Taffeta Publications, Brighton, East Sussex, England.

ISBN 0 9512835 4 5

All rights reserved. No part of this publication may be reproduced, stored in a retrieval system, or transmitted, in any form or by any means, electronic, mechanical, photocopying, recording or otherwise, without the prior permission of the copyright owner.

CONTENTS

Introduction		4
Sewing Hints		5
POPPET	Dress with two-tiered skirt, Hat and Knickers	8
SIMON & HALBIG	Low waisted Dress, pleated Hat, Petticoat & Drawers	10
ELIZABETH	Dress with gathered waist, gathered Hat, Petticoat & Drawers	14
CAROLINE	Princess-line Dress with pleats, brimmed Hat, Petticoat & Drawers	17
SWEET WILLIAM	Sailor Jacket and Trousers, Beret and Shirt	20
BLUE STOCKINGS	Low waisted Dress, ruched Hat, Petticoat & Drawers	23
YELLOW BOOTS	Bloused Dress with pleated front, Hat with brim, Petticoat & Drawers	26
HILDA	Christening Gown, Cape, Bonnet, Petticoat and Training Pants	29
General Information about Patterns and Conversion Table		32
Pattern pieces for all outfits		33 to 52

INTRODUCTION

First of all, I wish to express my grateful thanks to my dollmaker friends who kindly made the little all-bisque dolls especially for inclusion in this book.

Poppet by Gillie Taylor.
Little Heirlooms Simon & Halbig by Valerie Kay.
Elizabeth by Sonia Turner.
Caroline by Paul Jago of Recollect Studios.
Sweet William by Anne Lim.
Blue Stockings by Sandra Everett.
Yellow Boots by Sonia Turner.
Hilda by Margaret Tauschwitz.

Except for Poppet, a modern design from Dollies Galore International, the other dolls are either Kestner or Simon & Halbig German reproduction antique dolls, and I have identified them by their current popular names.

There is a colour photograph of each doll showing the clothes in close-up detail. The underwear though is mainly out of sight.

Making-up instructions for each garment are given in detail. There is a list of the fabric, lace, trimmings and notions you will require for each outfit.

Beside each photograph of the dressed doll, I have listed the basic measurements of the doll when undressed. You will then know whether a particular pattern will be suitable to make clothes for another doll of similar measurements.

All the patterns are grouped together at the back of the book. The pattern for each doll is easily identified by the doll's name on each pattern piece and also the relevant pages. Trace round each outline so that the book can remain intact. Transfer all markings and identification text to your copy pattern.

SEWING HINTS

Seam allowance
The seam allowance included in each pattern piece should be followed exactly so that the finished garment will be a perfect fit. You will notice that the underwear has a finer seam allowance than some of the main outfits.

Because of the small seams and little pieces of fabric with which you are working, it is easier to sew by hand. I have handsewn all of these little clothes except for adding the gathering threads with my sewing machine.

Gathers
Use your sewing machine with a slightly smaller stitch length than the largest machine stitch usually selected. Run two rows of gathers - one just above and the other just below any seam allowance. The resulting gathers are much smaller and suit the small scale of these little all-bisque dolls. A finer weight of fabric is also gathered with a fuller effect on this smaller stitch. Draw up the gathering threads as tightly as possible. Press over the fullness to set the folds between the two rows. Ease out the gathers to fit. (You will be able to move the gathers very easily with a pin.) Using this method you have a flatter edge to work with, instead of having to draw up the gathers after pinning the edge to a joining straight edge.

Stitch between the two rows of gathers to hold the tiny folds. The lower gathering thread, visible on the right side after the seam has been stitched, is then removed.

Sleeves
As most small-scale bodices have a side seam, sleeves are easier to fit into an open armhole while the bodice is still out flat after joining shoulder seams. The lower edge of the sleeve is also easier to decorate at this stage. The sleeve and side seam is then

joined in one operation. The seam edge of the sleeve will need to be neatened. A long straight sleeve, such as for a jacket, can present a problem when dressing a doll with a curved arm. The back edge of the underarm seam needs to be slightly longer than the front edge. The extra back length is eased at the elbow to fit the front edge. The sleeve seam then fits the inner arm and the extra fullness accommodates the bent elbow. The jacket sleeve for Sweet William shows how this is constructed.

Underwear
With such small necks and shoulders, adding lace to a neckline or around an armhole can sometimes be too bulky. On all the petticoat bodices in this book I have made very narrow hems to finish these edges. You could, however, oversew the raw edges and work a couple of rows of crochet with a fine hook and 100 gauge thread to decorate or work the crochet over the narrow hem. When joining a petticoat bodice to a skirt, the skirt opening will overlap and form a narrow pleat at the back of the skirt.

Fastenings
You will need very small buttons to fasten these little garments so that the doll can be dressed and undressed. However, sewing buttonholes to suit such small items can try your patience, especially when the opening edges have such narrow facings !

To make it easier to handle such a small starting loop, I insert closed small pointed embroidery scissors into the loop to hold the shape. I then slide my needle under the loop against the shiny edge of the scissors and so maintain an even tension for the first half of the buttonhole. When I have worked enough stitches to hold the loop, I then remove the scissors and finish the buttonhole quite easily.

Suppliers
Several doll haberdashery outlets have tiny buttons, narrow braid and ribbon. *The UK Doll Directory,* published by Hugglets, PO Box 290, Brighton, England, BN2 IDR, lists many of these haberdashery suppliers. You will also find details of the dollmakers who made the eight dolls included in this book.

POPPET

A Dollies Galore International design. An all-bisque doll with unique limb jointing.

Pattern to fit this doll or a doll of similar measurements:

Head to toe:	12.5cm
Across front chest:	2.5cm
Waist:	7cm
Hips:	9cm
Centre front neck to crutch:	5.5cm
Crutch to knee:	1cm
Inner arm - armhole to elbow:	1cm
Head (over wig):	
Ear to ear - front:	4.5cm
Ear to ear - back:	4cm
Centre crown - front to back:	4cm

Poppet is wearing a cap-sleeved Dress with a two-tiered skirt, a lace trimmed Hat and matching Knickers.

Please refer to Page 33 for the pattern pieces to make this outfit.

Materials required:

Dress, Hat and Pants:
    Fine cotton: 20cm x 23cm.
    Narrow Lace: Bodice: 10cm
                               Skirt: 40cm
                               Pants: 10cm
                               Hat: 26cm

2 small buttons.
Narrow elastic.

To make up
Seam Allowance on pattern pieces:
Bodice, Knickers & Hat - 4cm. Skirt - 7mm

Dress
Bodice:
With right sides together, stitch the two bodice pieces along back edges and around neck. Stitch outer edges keeping shape of cap sleeve. Pull bodice to right side through back free edges. Press. Add narrow lace flat along outer edges, following shape of cap sleeve.

At lower edge fold lace corners to right side of bodice and stitch down. At waistline only, oversew front to back to form armhole and create a bodice edge for skirt.

The skirt and overskirt are prepared separately and joined only by the top gathers.

For each skirt: Join back seam leaving 2.5cm open at top. Narrow hem opening. Turn up narrow hem at lower edge. Add lace flat to right side of hem allowing scalloped edge to extend beyond hem edge. Place overskirt on top of skirt matching back edges. Run two row of gathers along top edge. With right sides together, join skirts to bodice, back edges even. Adjust gathers and stitch seam. Press seam towards bodice. Oversew edge.

Add handworked loops to neck and waist edges of left back. Match buttons on right back. Add a ribbon bow to front waistline.

Knickers

Narrow hem along shaped leg. Add lace to match dress.
Join side seams.
Make a narrow hem at top edge for casing, leaving opening at back. Thread shirring elastic through casing. Secure elastic firmly.

Hat

Fold length in half and press. Open out and join back seam. Refold circle. Run gathers to hold double raw edge. Draw up tightly and secure thread firmly.

Fold back seam 7mm towards wrong side to form a straight back edge. Stitch folded section to wrong side.

Gather remaining edge of circle, 7mm in from outer edge to form a frilled brim. Add lace to inside front gathers to extend slightly beyond edge. Continue lace around back straight edge.

Add a small circle of lace to centre crown to hide gathers. Decorate centre lace with a ribbon bow to hang down at back.

SIMON & HALBIG DOLL
An all-bisque reproduction German doll from Little Heirlooms, Staffordshire.

Pattern to fit this doll or a doll of similar measurements:

Head to toe:	12.5cm
Across front chest:	3.25cm
Waist:	8.75cm
Hips:	9.5cm
Centre front neck to crutch:	5.75cm
Crutch to knee:	1.25cm
Inner arm - armhole to elbow:	2cm
Head (over wig)	
Ear to ear - front:	6.25cm
Ear to ear - back:	5.75cm
Centre crown - front to back:	6.25cm

This small Simon & Halbig doll is wearing a low-waisted Dress and Hat with pleated brim. Underneath she has a low waisted Petticoat and Drawers.

Please refer to Pages 34 and 35 for the pattern pieces to make this outfit.

Materials required:

Dress & Hat:	Silk piece:	23cm x 56cm
	Cotton lining:	10cm x 30cm
	Narrow lace:	110cm
	Narrow braid:	50cm
	2mm ribbon:	20cm
Petticoat and Drawers:	Cotton lawn:	23cm x 26cm
	Narrow lace:	40cm
	Straight lace:	6cm
	Small buttons:	2
	Narrow cord:	15cm

To make up

Seam allowance on pattern pieces: 4mm

Dress

Stitch dress and lining separately. Join back seam. Join shoulder seams. Tack main fabric facing to front lining sections.

Sleeve (unlined): Make a box pleat down centre along lines indicated. Tack top and bottom edges. Join one edge of sleeveband to sleeve. Decorate sleeveband seam with narrow braid.
Attach sleevehead to dress armhole while flat. Ease fullness at shoulder line. Oversew raw edges.

Join side, sleeve and band in one operation. Turn band to wrong side and hem in place. Join side seams of lining. Oversew lining armholes to neaten.

With right sides together, join dress to lining around outer edge, matching seams and edges. Trim corners and turn to right side.

and press. Stitch lining armhole to oversewn edge of sleeve armhole.

Fold right front along foldline to form a long rever. Fold top corner of left front to right side of dress to form neckline. Press.

Add narrow braid to edge of long rever, around neck and along top folded corner. Add lace just under fold of rever, around neck and under top folded corner.

Overlap front sections until the bottom edge is even with the back. Pin overlapped edges. Oversew lower edge to neaten and hold front overlap. Knife pleat a length of lace to fit lower edge of dress. Attach pleated lace so that scalloped edge extends just beyond dress edge.

Skirt pleated frill:
Fold length in half and press. Make knife pleats along folded length to fit lower edge of dress. Press. Open out pleat edges and stitch back seam. Reform pleats. Oversew raw edges to hold pleats.

Place oversewn edge of frill to bottom of dress so that frill edge matches extended edge of pleated lace. Stitch frill in place.

Cover top of pleats with another length of knife-pleated lace. Cover edge of attached lace with narrow braid. Add a small ribbon bow at base of rever.

Please note: The overlapping fronts are not fastened.

Hat

Fold length in half and press. Open out and stitch back seam. Reform circle. Oversew raw edges at outer edge. Add knife-pleated lace over oversewn edge.

Gather along folded edge for centre crown. Draw up tightly and fasten securely.

Fold brim in half and press. Make knife pleats along length to fit outer edge of hat. Open out end pleats and stitch back seam. Reform pleats. Oversew raw edges to hold pleats. Place pleated brim just above pleated lace and stitch in place. Cover oversewn edge of brim with knife-pleated lace.

Add a ribbon bow at back of hat to fall over brim.

Petticoat

Bodice:
Fold under and hem facings of back sections. Narrow hem centre edges of front bodice. Add narrow straight lace to either edge to join front sections and decorate.

Join shoulder seams. Narrow hem neckline and also armholes. Join side seams. Overlap back facings and stitch across lower edge.

Skirt:
Join back seam.
Narrow hem lower edge and add lace flat over hem. Gather along top edge.
With right sides together, join bodice to skirt.

Adjust gathers. Stitch seam. Oversew raw edges and press seam towards bodice.

Add handworked loops to neck and waist edges of left back. Match buttons on right back.

Drawers

Narrow hem leg edges. Make narrow tuck above hem. Add narrow lace over hem.
Join back seam.
Join inner leg seam.

Fold under casing at top edge. Hem in place leaving opening at back. Thread narrow cord through casing.

ELIZABETH
An all-bisque reproduction German doll.

Pattern to fit this doll or a doll of similar measurements:

Head to toe:	14cm
Across front chest:	3.25cm
Waist:	8.25cm
Hips:	8.75cm
Centre front neck to crutch:	5.75cm
Crutch to knee:	1.25cm
Inner arm - armhole to elbow:	2cm
Head (over wig)	
Ear to ear - front:	6.25cm
Ear to ear - back:	5cm
Centre crown - front to back:	5.75cm

Elizabeth is wearing a Dress with tucked and embroidered bodice and gathered skirt, a gathered Hat, and underneath she has lace edged Petticoat and Drawers.

Please refer to Pages 36 and 37 for the pattern pieces to make this outfit.

Materials required:

Dress & Hat:	Cotton print:	18cm x 36cm
	Narrow lace:	60cm
	Small buttons:	2
	7mm Ribbon:	20cm
	Embroidery thread.	
Petticoat	Cotton lawn:	18cm x 30cm
and Drawers:	Straight lace:	5cm
	Scallop lace:	45cm
	Small buttons:	2
	Narrow cord:	15cm

To make up
Seam Allowance on pattern pieces:
Bodice, & Underwear - 4cm. Skirt - 7mm

Dress
Please note: Bodice front has miniature tucks formed by whipping the edge of a fold instead of working small running stitches.

Bodice: Make first tuck by whipping centre front fold. Stitch 4 more tucks in the same way along lines indicated. Turn under facings on back sections and hem. Join shoulder seams.

Oversew raw edge of lower sleeve. Add lace to oversewn edge. Gather top of sleeve. Fit into armhole. Adjust fullness and stitch seam. Join sleeve and side seam. Gather along lace straight edge to draw up sleeve to fit over the doll's hand.

Oversew neck edge. Add slightly gathered lace to wrong side of neck. Bring lace to right side and stitch just below neck edge to hold frill in place.

Skirt: Join back seam of skirt, leaving 2.5cm open at top. Hem opening edges to neaten. Make 1.25cm hem at lower edge. Run two rows of gathers along top edge. Join skirt to bodice matching back edges. Adjust gathers. Stitch seam. Press seam towards bodice.

Add buttonhole loops to right back facing at neck and waist. Add buttons to match on left back. Decorate centre front bodice with French knots between tucks. Ribbon sash optional.

Hat
Join outer edge of two crown sections, leaving small gap at back. Pull crown to right side and close gap. Add lace to top and inside of curved edge only, having lace edge extending over hat.

Run gathers around hat, including straight back edge, following straight edge of attached lace. Draw up to fit doll's head. (approx. 9cm circumference). Fasten thread securely. Add a bow into front gathers.

Petticoat
Bodice: Turn facings on back sections and hem. Make a narrow hem on either side of centre front. Add straight lace to these edges to join centre front sections and decorate. Join shoulder seams. Narrow hem neckline and armhole edges. Join side seams.

Skirt: Oversew lower edge. Add narrow lace to oversewn edge. Join back seam, leaving 2.5cm open at top. Narrow hem opening edges. Run 2 rows of gathers along top edge. Join skirt to bodice, matching back edges. Adjust gathers. Stitch seam. Press seam towards bodice.
Add handworked loops to neck and waist edges of left back. Match buttons on right back.

Drawers
Narrow hem leg edges. Add narrow lace over hem. Join back seam. Join inner leg seam.
Turn under casing at top and hem to wrong side, leaving small gap at back. Thread narrow cord for ties through casing.

CAROLINE

An all-bisque reproduction German Kestner doll with googly eyes.

Pattern to fit this doll or a doll of similar measurements:

Head to toe:	15.5cm
Across front chest:	4.5cm
Waist:	12cm
Hips:	13.75cm
Centre front: neck to crutch:	7.5cm
Crutch to knee:	2.5cm
Armhole to elbow:	1.25cm
Head (over wig)	
Ear to ear - front:	10cm
Ear to ear - back:	8.75cm
Centre crown - front to back	8.75cm

Caroline is wearing a princess-line Dress with two inverted pleats at front and back, and a matching Hat with turned-back brim. Underneath she has lace trimmed Petticoat and Drawers.

Please refer to Pages 38 and 39 for the pattern pieces to make this outfit.

Materials required:

Dress & Hat:	Cotton print:	18cm x 36cm
	Narrow lace:	40cm
	7mm Ribbon:	50cm
	Hooks:	3
Petticoat & Drawers:	Cotton lawn:	18cm x 30cm
	Narrow lace:	60cm
	Small buttons:	2
	Narrow cord:	15cm

To make up
Seam allowance on pattern pieces:
Dress & Petticoat skirt - 7mm
Petticoat bodice and Drawers: - 4mm

Dress
Join lower pleat extensions. Join upper bodice seams. Press each pleat foldline. On right side bring pleats to meet in centre. On wrong side oversew top of extension to neaten. Turn full length facings on back sections and hem. Join shoulder seams.

Oversew neck edge. Add a lace frill around neck. Overlap back facings. Add three buttonhole loops and buttons to match at neck, waist and halfway down skirt.

Narrow hem lower edge of sleeve and add narrow lace. Ease sleevehead to fit armhole and stitch seam. Join sleeve and side seams. Make a 7mm hem at lower edge.

Cut two 25cm lengths of ribbon for ties. Make a bow at one end of tie and secure bow to top of each front pleat. Tie at back.

Hat
(Use 'Yellow Boots' Hat Crown and Brim pattern pieces to be found on Page 47.)

Crown: Tack lining to crown. Run two rows of gathers around outer edge. Mark the quarter points of outer edge with pins ready to join the brim. Draw up gathers tightly and press over gathers to set the folds.

Brim: Join back seam of each brim section. Join outer edges of brim, matching back seams. Bring to right side and press.

Staystitch seamline of inner circle. Snip seam allowance as marked. Turn under seam allowance of one edge and mark the other edge with pins for the quarter points.

Join this edge to gathered crown, matching the quarter points. Adjust gathers and stitch seam. Hem folded edge of brim over seam on wrong side.

Add a ribbon band over brim seam and tie a bow at back.

Petticoat
Bodice:
Turn facings of back sections and hem. Join shoulder seams. Stitch 4mm hem around neckline and armhole edges. Join side seams.

Skirt:
Join back seam leaving 4 cm open at top. Make 2cm hem at lower edge. Run two rows of gathers along top edge. Join bodice to skirt, matching back edges. Adjust gathers. Stitch seam. Press seam towards bodice.

Add two buttonhole loops and buttons to back facings to fasten.

Drawers
Oversew leg edges. Add narrow lace to oversewn edge. Join front seam. Join inner leg seam. Turn casing along top edge to wrong side and hem, leaving gap to thread narrow cord for ties.

SWEET WILLIAM
An all-bisque reproduction German doll with molded hair.

Pattern to fit this doll or a doll of similar measurements:

Head to toe:	18cm
Across front chest:	5cm
Waist:	12cm
Hips:	12.5cm
Centre front neck to crutch:	7.5cm
Crutch to knee:	2.5cm
Inner arm: - armhole to elbow:	2.5cm
Head (over wig)	
Ear to ear - front:	8.75cm
Ear to ear - back:	7.5cm
Centre crown - front to back:	7.5cm

Sweet William is wearing a Sailor Jacket with a navy edged sailor collar and matching Trousers and Beret. Underneath he has a sleeveless Shirt, buttoned at the back.

Please refer to Pages 40 and 41 for the pattern pieces to make this outfit.

Materials required:

Jacket, Trousers and Beret:	Blue cotton:	22cm x 60cm
	7mm ribbon:	45cm
	Narrow elastic:	20cm
Collar:	White Cotton:	8cm x 10cm
	4mm Navy ribbon:	40cm
Shirt:	White Cotton:	13cm x 25cm
	Small buttons:	2

To make up
Seam allowance on pattern pieces: 7mm

Sailor Jacket
Join shoulder seams. Ease sleevehead into armhole and stitch seam. Make 7mm hem at wrist edge of sleeve. Join side and sleeve seam, easing fullness at back elbow, and matching armhole and wrist edges. Neaten hem edge. Turn to right side.

Stitch back facing to facing extention of front sections. Stitch back facing to back jacket at neck edge. Oversew facing raw edges. Fold facings to wrong side. Mitre at V to form neckline slant. Do not stitch facing down on wrong side but catch at shoulders.
Make a 7mm hem at lower edge.

Collar
Join outer edge of collar sections. Turn to right side and press. Add two rows of narrow navy ribbon to right side of collar. Bind collar neckline with a narrow bias strip of matching fabric. Leave short neatened extensions of binding at front edges.

Place collar over jacket, matching neckline. Stitch in place through binding seamline. Bring binding extentions at ends of collar to wrong side and stitch to facing.

Add a ribbon bow to hold fronts in place at end of collar.

(Jacket can fall open unfastened or overlap with a button and buttonhole.)

Trousers
Oversew raw edges of lower legs.
Join front seam.
Join back seam.
Join inner leg seam.

At leg ends fold 7mm towards wrong side and hem oversewn edge in place.

Make a casing at top along foldline. Hem in place. Leave small gap at back seam.

Thread narrow elastic through casing and fasten securely.

Shirt
Narrow hem facings at back edges. Stitch a narrow hem around neckline and armholes.
Join side seams.
Bind lower edge to neaten.
Work buttonhole loops to top and bottom of back facings and add buttons to match.

Beret
Tack lining to crown and gather around outer edge. With pins mark the quarter points around outer edge.
Fold under seam allowance along one edge of headband and press. Join headband into a circle. With pins, mark the quarter points along other edge of headband. Stitch headband to crown, matching pins and adjusting gathers evenly. Fold headband in half and hem to inside.

Add a ribbon bow to one side of headband.

BLUE STOCKINGS
An all-bisque reproduction Simon & Halbig Doll. She is known by this name because, for authenticity, her long socks are always painted blue.

Pattern to fit this doll or a doll of similar measurements:

Head to toe:	20cm
Across front chest:	3.75cm
Waist:	12cm
Hips:	12.5cm
Centre front neck to crutch:	8.25cm
Crutch to knee:	2.5cm
Inner arm - armhole to elbow:	2.5cm
Head (over wig)	
Ear to ear - front:	7.5cm
Ear to ear - back:	6.25cm
Centre crown - front to back:	6.25cm

Blue Stockings is wearing a low waisted Dress with a short pleated skirt and matching Hat with a lace edged ruched crown. Underneath she has lace edged Petticoat and Drawers.

Please refer to Pages 42, 43 and 44 for the pattern pieces to make this outfit.

Materials required:

Dress & Hat:
- Silk fabric: 23cm x 80cm
- 7mm Lace: 90cm
- Lace front: 7.5cm x 10cm
- (extra 12cm for lace sleeves)
- Skirt Lining: 65cm x 4.5cm
- 4cm Skirt Lace: 65cm

Petticoat & Drawers:
- Cotton Lawn: 40cm x 25cm
- 7mm Lace: 30cm
- Small buttons: 2
- Narrow cord: 25cm

To make up

Seam allowance on pattern pieces: - 7mm
Except Petticoat bodice and drawers: - 4mm
Please note: Back of Dress is open full length and overlaps from neck to hem.

Dress

Bodice (unlined): Turn facings on back sections and hem. Join shoulder seams. Sleeves: *If using lace,* oversew raw edge of dress armhole to neaten.
If using fabric, narrow hem lower edge. Stitch sleevehead into armhole. Oversew raw edges. Join side and sleeve seam. Oversew neck edge. Add a lace frill to neckline.

Skirt: Join lining to skirt along bottom edge. Bring to right side and match raw edges of top. (Small hem will form on wrong side.) Neaten side edges.

Knife pleat skirt length to match lower edge of bodice. Join skirt to bodice, matching back edges. Add pleated lace to inside of skirt to match depth of skirt. (If necessary, join narrower lace to create the correct depth).

On right side decorate front bodice with a piece of deep lace. Draw lace together at neckline and spread decorative edge to finish over low waistline. Cover edges of applied lace with narrow lace. Continue lace along low waistline to back edges. Add same lace to edges of fabric sleeves. Add hooks and buttonhole loops to back facings. Fringe raw edge of single fabric bow and add band at centre. Attach at back waistline.

Hat

Crown: Join one back crown to crown and the other to lining. Join hat to lining around outer edge, leaving gap at centre back. Pull to right side, close gap and press.

Ruched Top: Fold under top and bottom of this section and press. Run a gathering thread along top and bottom raw edges to hold folds in place. Fold section in half and run a gathering thread to form a centre tuck. Pull all three threads to draw up gathers to fit hat crown. Secure thread firmly. Place ruched section over crown with front frill overlapping edge and back frill overlapping back crown. Fit to either side with a centre tuck to reduce fullness. Stitch ruched section in place through gathers. Neaten side edges. Add pleated lace around inner edge of hat. Fringe edges of single bow and tie in a knot. Attach bow at lower edge of back crown.

Petticoat

Bodice: Turn facing of back sections to inside and hem. Narrow hem neck and armhole edges. Join side seams.

Skirt: Join back seam leaving 4cm open at top. Neaten opening edges. Make a 2cm hem at lower edge. Make three 4mm tucks above hem. Stitch lace flat over hem. Run two rows of gathers along top edge. Join skirt to bodice, matching back edges, adjusting gathers. Stitch seam. Add loops and buttons to fasten back bodice.

Drawers

Make 4mm hem at leg edges. Stitch lace over hem. Make a 4mm tuck above hem. Stitch front and back seams. Stitch inner leg seam. Turn casing to wrong side and hem, leaving gap to thread narrow cord.

YELLOW BOOTS

An all bisque reproduction German Kestner Doll. She is known by this name because, for authenticity, her distinctive molded boots are always painted yellow.

Pattern to fit this doll or a doll of similar measurements:

Head to toe:	21.5cm
Across front chest:	5.75cm
Waist:	12.5cm
Hips:	13.75cm
Centre front neck to crutch:	10cm
Crutch to knee:	2.5cm
Inner arm - armhole to elbow:	3.25cm
Head (over wig)	
Ear to ear - front:	11.5cm
Ear to ear - back:	8.75cm
Centre crown - front to back:	9.5cm

Yellow Boots is wearing a bloused Dress with pleats on front bodice and skirt. Her hat has a gathered crown and wide brim. Underneath she is wearing a lace edged frilled Petticoat and a pair of Drawers gathered into legbands edged with lace.

Please refer to Pages 45, 46, 47 and 48 for the pattern pieces to make this outfit.

Materials required:

Dress & Hat:
- Silk fabric — 23cm x 80 cm
- 7mm Lace: — 45cm
- 13mm Ribbon: — 90cm
- Hooks: — 4

Petticoat & Drawers:
- Cotton Lawn: — 46cm x 23cm
- 7mm Lace: — 60cm
- Small buttons: — 2
- Narrow cord: — 40cm
- Embroidery thread

To make up
Seam allowance on pattern pieces: - 7mm
Except Petticoat Bodice and drawers: - 4mm

Dress
Bodice: Turn facings on back sections to inside and hem. Form pleats in front section and press. Outline pleat folds with small running stitches on outside and inside. Stitch pleats in place at top and bottom. Join shoulder seams. Oversew raw edge of neck to neaten. Add gathered lace to wrong side of neck edge. Bring to right side and stitch just below neckline to form a frill.

Sleeve: Make a 4mm turning along lower edge. Add lace over right and wrong sides of turned edge. Gather sleevehead. Fit into armhole. Adjust fullness. Stitch seam. Join sleeve and side seam. Run gathers along top of lace and draw up to fit doll's arm.

Skirt: (N.B. Pattern piece needs to be widened by 5cm) Make pleats in front and tack in place. Press. Join back seam to X. Neaten opening edges. Run 2 rows of gathers along top from pleats to back edges. Join skirt to bodice, matching centre front and back edges. Adjust gathers. Stitch seam. Press seam towards bodice.

Add 4 buttonhole loops and hooks to back bodice. Add ribbon sash around waistline.

When doll is dressed the sash will hold the bloused fullness of the bodice.

Hat
Crown: Tack lining to crown. Run two rows of gathers around outer edge. Mark the quarter points of outer edge with pins ready to join the brim. Draw up gathers tightly and press over gathers to set the folds.
Brim: Join back seam of each brim section. Join outer edges of brim, matching back seams. Bring to right side and press. Staystitch seamline of inner circle. Snip seam allowance as marked. Turn under seam allowance of one edge and mark the other edge with pins for the quarter points.

Join this edge to gathered crown, matching the quarter points. Adjust gathers and stitch seam. Hem folded edge of brim over seam on wrong side.
Add a ribbon band over brim seam and tie a bow at back.

Petticoat
Bodice: Turn under facings of back sections and hem. Join shoulder seams. Make 4mm hem around neckline and armhole edges. Join side seams.
Skirt: Join back seam leaving 4cm open at top. Neaten opening edges. Run two rows of gathers along top edge. Stitch skirt to bodice, matching back edges and adjusting gathers.
Skirt frill: Join back seam. Oversew lower edge and add lace flat. Run two rows of gathers along top edge. Stitch frill to lower skirt, matching back seams and adjusting gathers. Press seams towards skirt. Add loops and buttons to back bodice. Decorate lower skirt with featherstitching just above frill.

Drawers
Gather leg edges. Join leg band to leg edge. Adjust gathers. Press seam towards band. Fold legband in half and hem over seam. Add narrow lace to folded edge of legband. Decorate band with featherstitching.
Join front seam. Join back seam. Join inner leg seam. Turn casing to wrong side and hem, leaving gap to thread narrow cord.

HILDA
An all-bisque reproduction German Kestner Character Baby Doll.

Pattern to fit this doll or a doll of similar measurements:

Head to toe:	20.25cm
Across front chest:	5cm
Waist:	13.25cm
Hips:	13.75cm
Centre front neck to crutch:	9.5cm
Crutch to knee:	2.5cm
Inner arm: - armhole to elbow:	2cm
Head (over wig)	
Ear to ear - front:	10cm
Ear to ear - back:	7cm
Centre crown - front to back:	8.75cm

Hilda is wearing a long Christening Gown, and Bonnet and a short Cape with collar. Underneath she has a long frilled Petticoat and authentic training pants.

Please refer to Pages 49, 50, 51 and 52 for the pattern pieces to make this outfit.

Materials required:

Dress & Bonnet:	Silk:	25.5cm x 115cm
	13mm Lace:	165cm
	2 small buttons	
	7mm Ribbon	30cm
Petticoat:	Cotton lawn:	18cm x 115cm
	7mm Lace:	92cm
	2 small buttons	
Training Pants:	Fleeced Cotton:	15cm x 15cm
	7mm silk ribbon:	61cm
	2 small buttons	
Cape:	Wool fabric:	26cm x 18cm
	Silk lining:	26cm x 18cm
	13mm Lace:	38cm
	7mm silk ribbon:	20cm

To make up
Seam allowance on pattern pieces: - 7mm
Except Petticoat Bodice and drawers: - 4mm

Long Dress   Turn under and hem back bodice facings. Cut fold of centre back from top to X. Neaten opening with a strip of straight fabric to form a placket. Run two rows of gathers along top edges of skirt. Join skirt to bodice, matching back facings with placket. Adjust gathers. Stitch seam.
Join front panel to side front edges.
Join shoulder seams.
Bind neck edge with a bias strip, 2cm wide x 13cm long.
Sleeves: Gather top and bottom edges of each sleeve. Join one edge of sleeveband to each sleeve. Press seam towards band. Turn under seam allowance of other edge of band and press. Join sleeve and band seam. Turn band to inside and hem folded edge over seamline. Decorate sleeveband with gathered lace. Add lace around neckline. Add lace flat down each side of front panel.   Skirt frill: Join length into a circle. Narrow hem lower edge. Make 2 narrow tucks 7mm apart, above

hem. Gather top edge. Stitch frill to lower edge of skirt. Press seam upwards.

Long Petticoat
Use Dress Front Panel for front and back sections. Cut down centre fold of back 6cm from top for opening. Join shoulder seams. Narrow hem around neck and back opening. Narrow hem each armhole. Join side seams.

Lower frill: Join length into a circle at back seam. Make a 4mm hem at lower edge. Add narrow lace over hem. Run 2 rows of gathers along top edge. Stitch frill to skirt, adjusting gathers. Add lace over seam.
Add buttons and loops to back neck edge.

Training Pants
Using 7mm wide coloured silk ribbon, attach one edge around outer edge, stitching 3mm in from edge. Fold ribbon to wrong side and stitch in place to form a bound edge. Attach a 8cm length of ribbon to either top corner for ties. Attach a button either side of front and make a buttonhole at each corner of long section, where indicated.

Cape
Stitch collar to collar lining around outer curve only. Turn collar to right side and press. Tack neck edges together. Decorate outer curve with braid. Place wrong side of collar to right side of cape, matching centre back. Tack in place.
Place cape lining over cape and collar and stitch around outer edge including neckline. Leave a small gap at lower back. Turn cape to right side and stitch gap to close. Press outer edges. Decorate edge with braid. Stitch ribbon ties to either side of front edge under collar.

Bonnet
Join back seam of bonnet and also lining. Join back crown to each bonnet and lining section. Stitch bonnet to lining around outer edge, leaving small gap at centre back. Turn bonnet to right side and close gap. Fold brim to right side along foldline.
Attach narrow lace to outer edge and around brim. Add lace around back crown circle to cover seam. Attach ribbon bows and ties to each front corner.

GENERAL INFORMATION ABOUT THE FOLLOWING PATTERN PIECES.

o A seam allowance is included in each pattern piece. and notified at the beginning of the making-up instructions.

o Each pattern piece is identified with the name of the doll. They are grouped together in separate sections on the following pages.

o The pattern pieces for the brimmed hat for Yellow Boots on Page 47 are also used for Caroline's hat.

o The crown pattern piece for the brimmed hat is used for Sweet William's sailor beret.

o Because of the need to identify the location of the front pleats, a full-size dress skirt pattern for Yellow Boots will not fit the page. Please note the instruction to widen the pattern by 5cm between the parallel lines.

o Some of the pieces needed to construct these clothes are given by measurement and are not drawn as an actual pattern. These are contained in small boxes.

o Identification text has been added to a pattern piece in such a way that it can be read the right way up when placed on the fabric. Trace around the pieces and transfer the text as necessary.

o The measurements of the doll, the measurements in the pattern boxes as well as any measurements mentioned in the making-up instructions are given in centimetres or millimetres.

o The following conversion into Inches will help those who prefer to work in Imperial rather than Metric measurement.

One-eight inch	4 mm
One-quarter inch	7 mm
One-half inch	1.25cm
Three-quarters inch	2 cm
One inch	2.5 cm
Two inches	5 cm
Three inches	7.5 cm
Four inches	10 cm
Five inches	12.5 cm
Six inches	15 cm
Seven inches	18 cm
Eight inches	20 cm
Nine inches	23 cm
Ten inches	25.5cm
Eleven inches	28cm
Twelve inches	30.5cm

... and so on ...

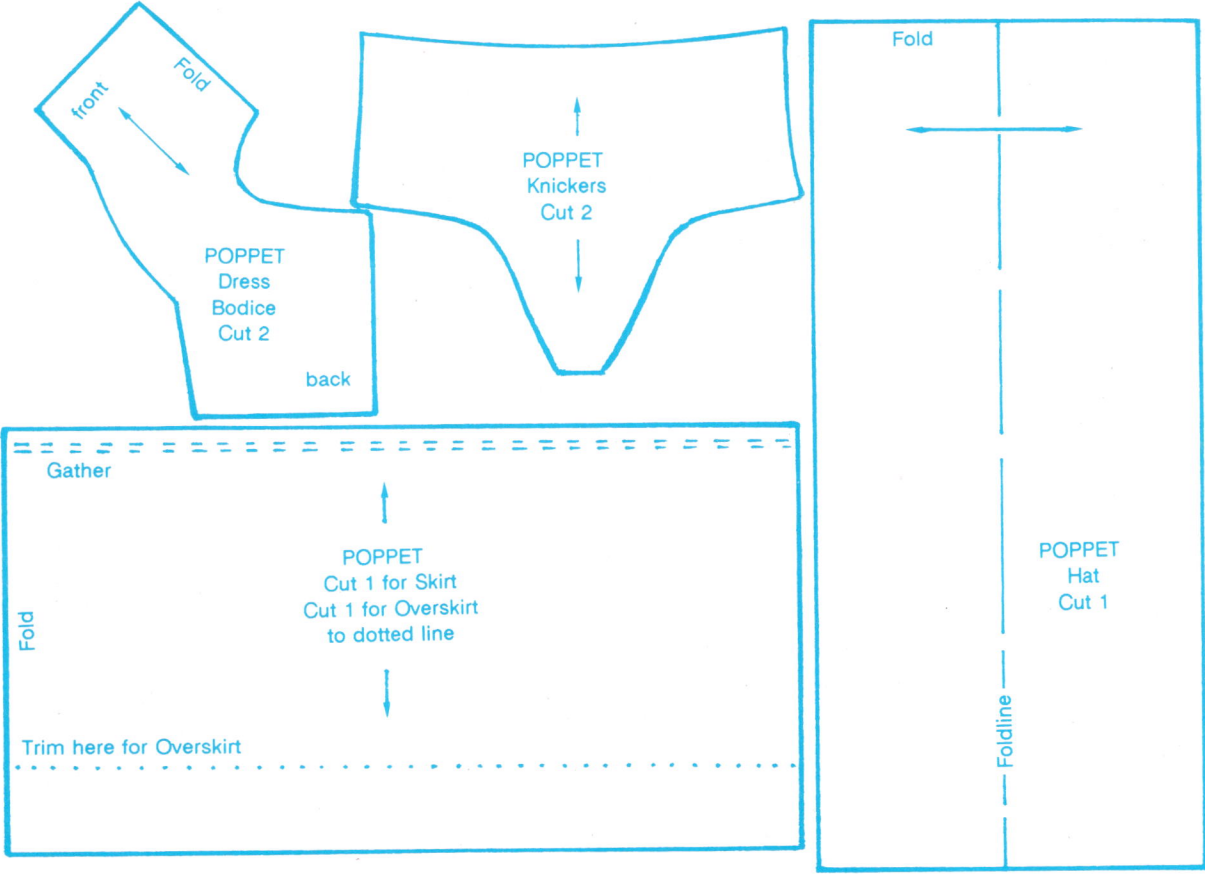

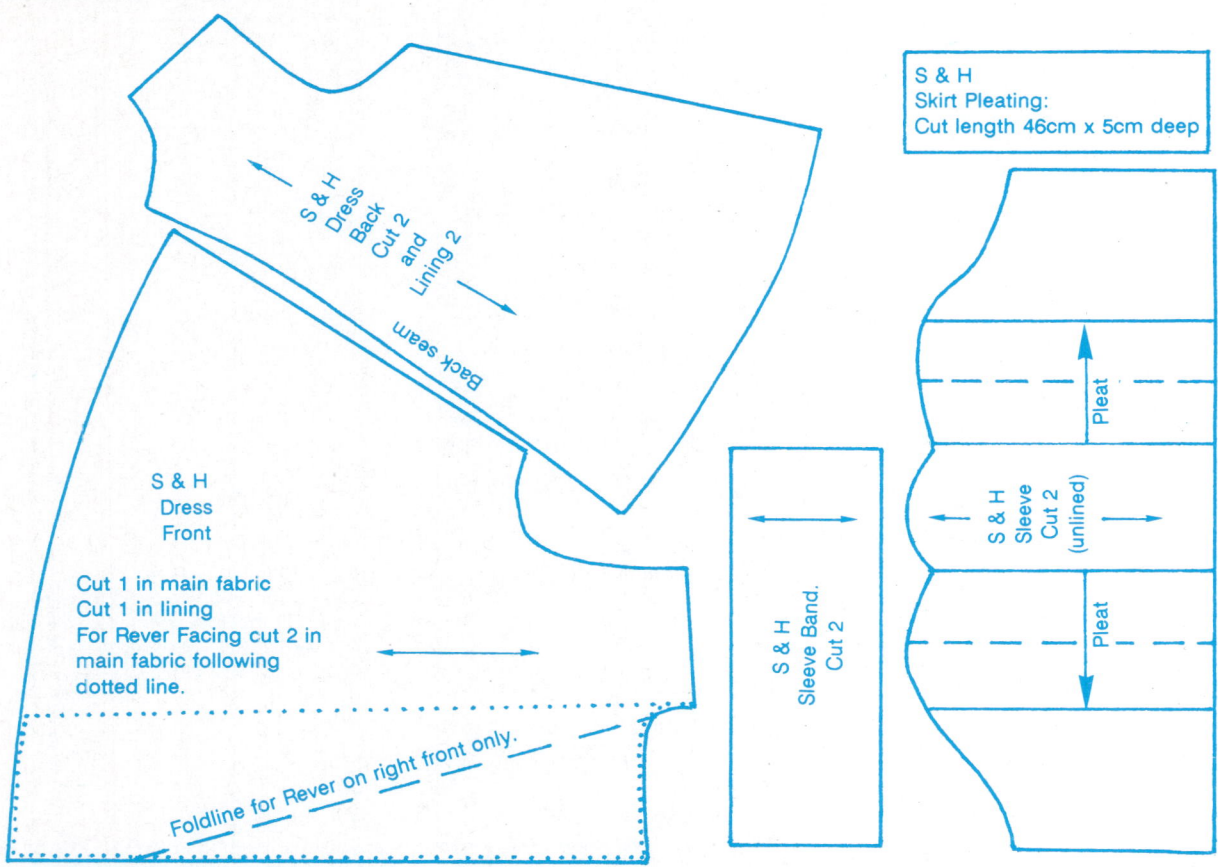

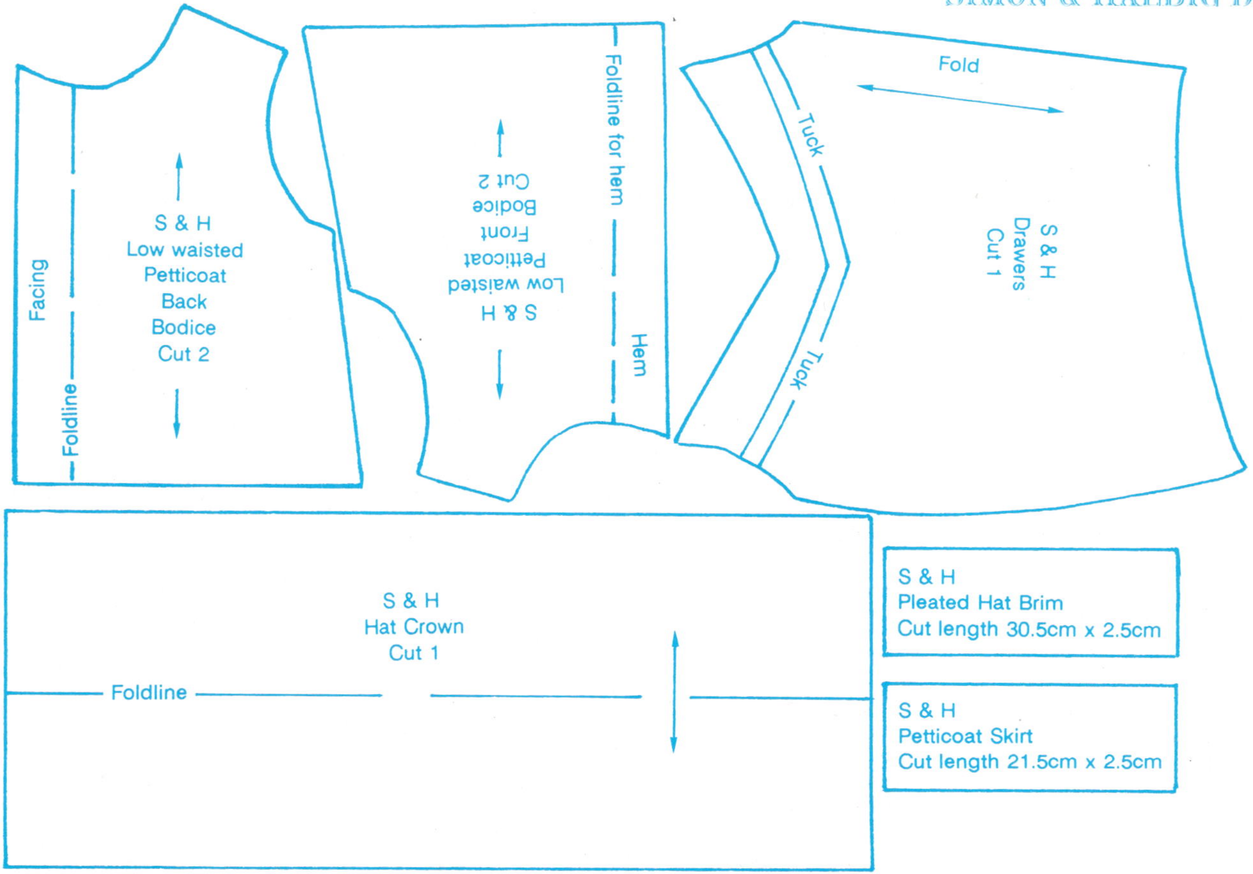

SIMON & HALBIG DOLL

S & H
Low waisted
Petticoat
Back
Bodice
Cut 2

Facing

Foldline

Foldline for hem

Hem

S & H
Low waisted
Petticoat
Front
Bodice
Cut 2

Fold

Tuck

Tuck

S & H
Drawers
Cut 1

S & H
Hat Crown
Cut 1

Foldline

S & H
Pleated Hat Brim
Cut length 30.5cm x 2.5cm

S & H
Petticoat Skirt
Cut length 21.5cm x 2.5cm

35

ELIZABETH

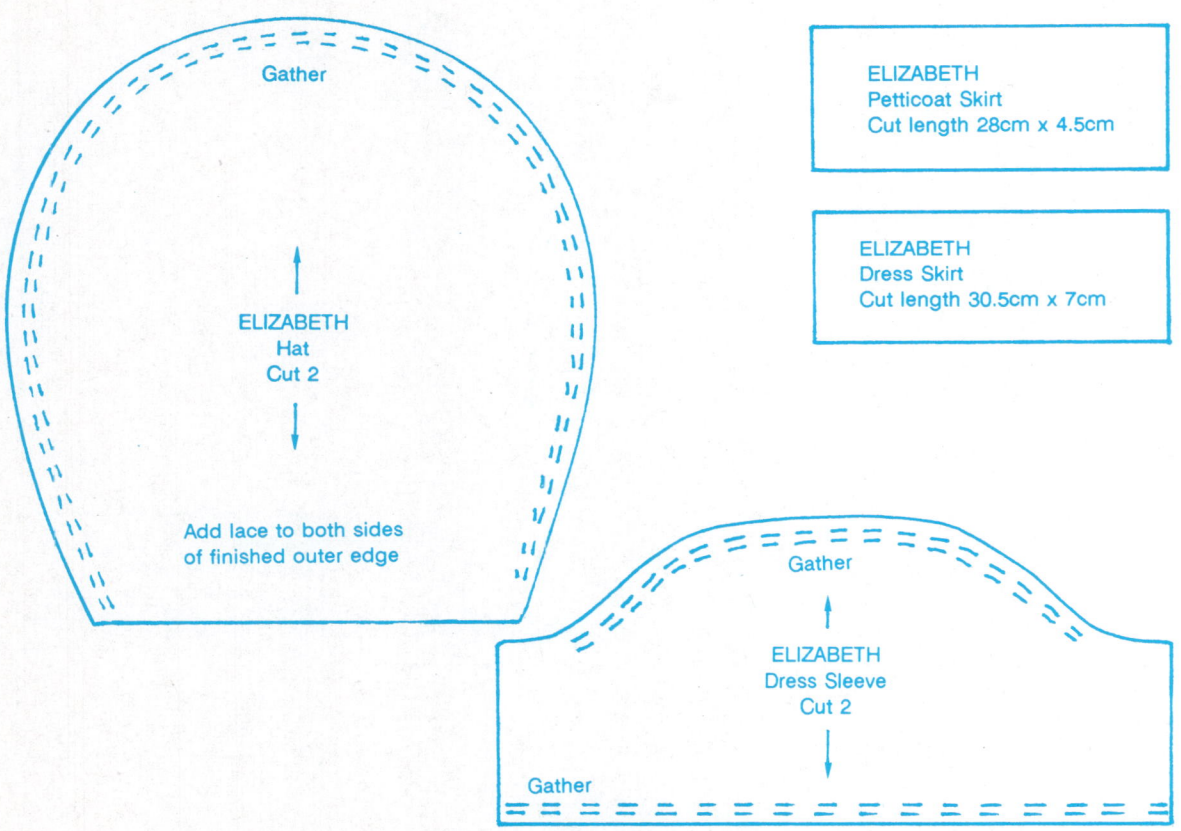

ELIZABETH

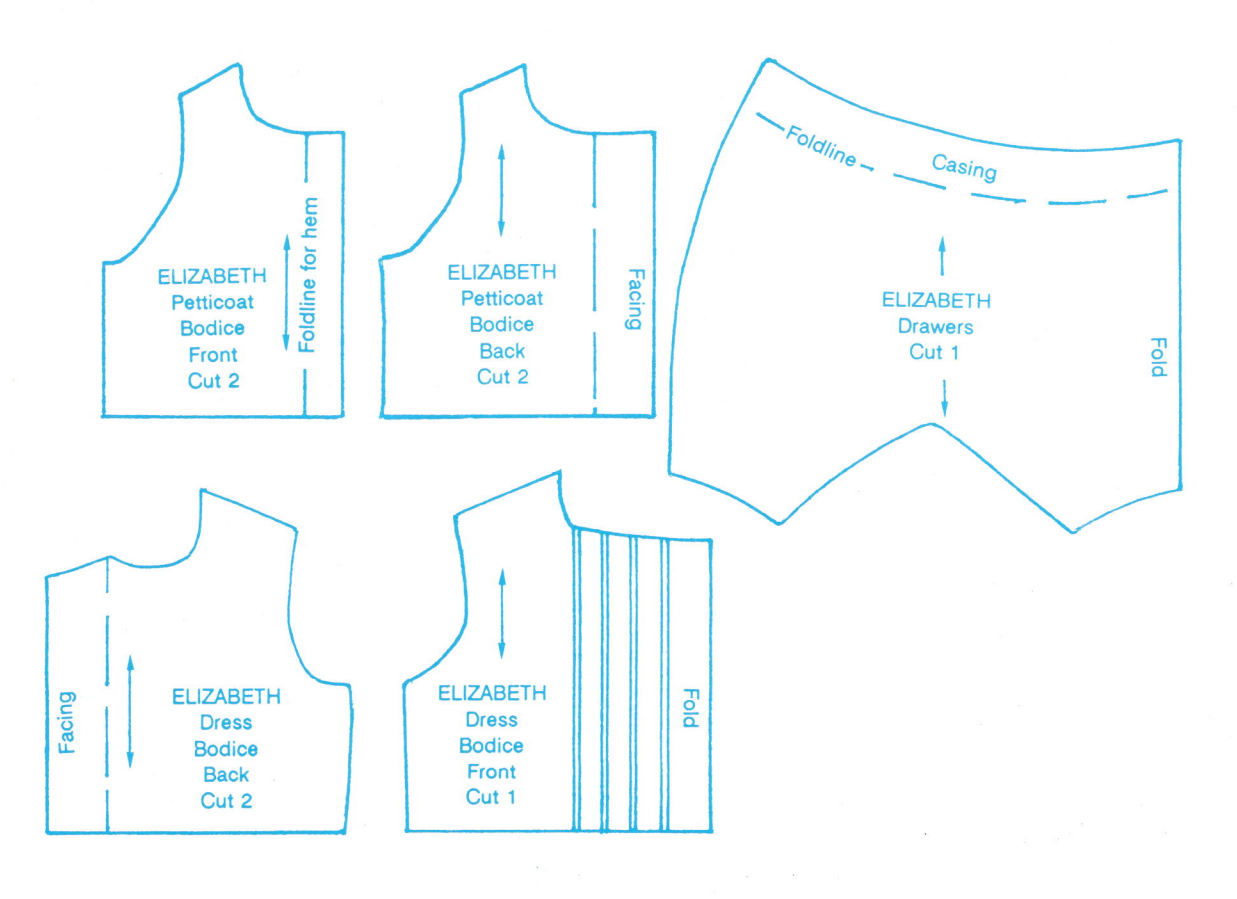

ELIZABETH
Petticoat
Bodice
Front
Cut 2

Foldline for hem

ELIZABETH
Petticoat
Bodice
Back
Cut 2

Facing

Foldline — Casing

ELIZABETH
Drawers
Cut 1

Fold

Facing

ELIZABETH
Dress
Bodice
Back
Cut 2

ELIZABETH
Dress
Bodice
Front
Cut 1

Fold

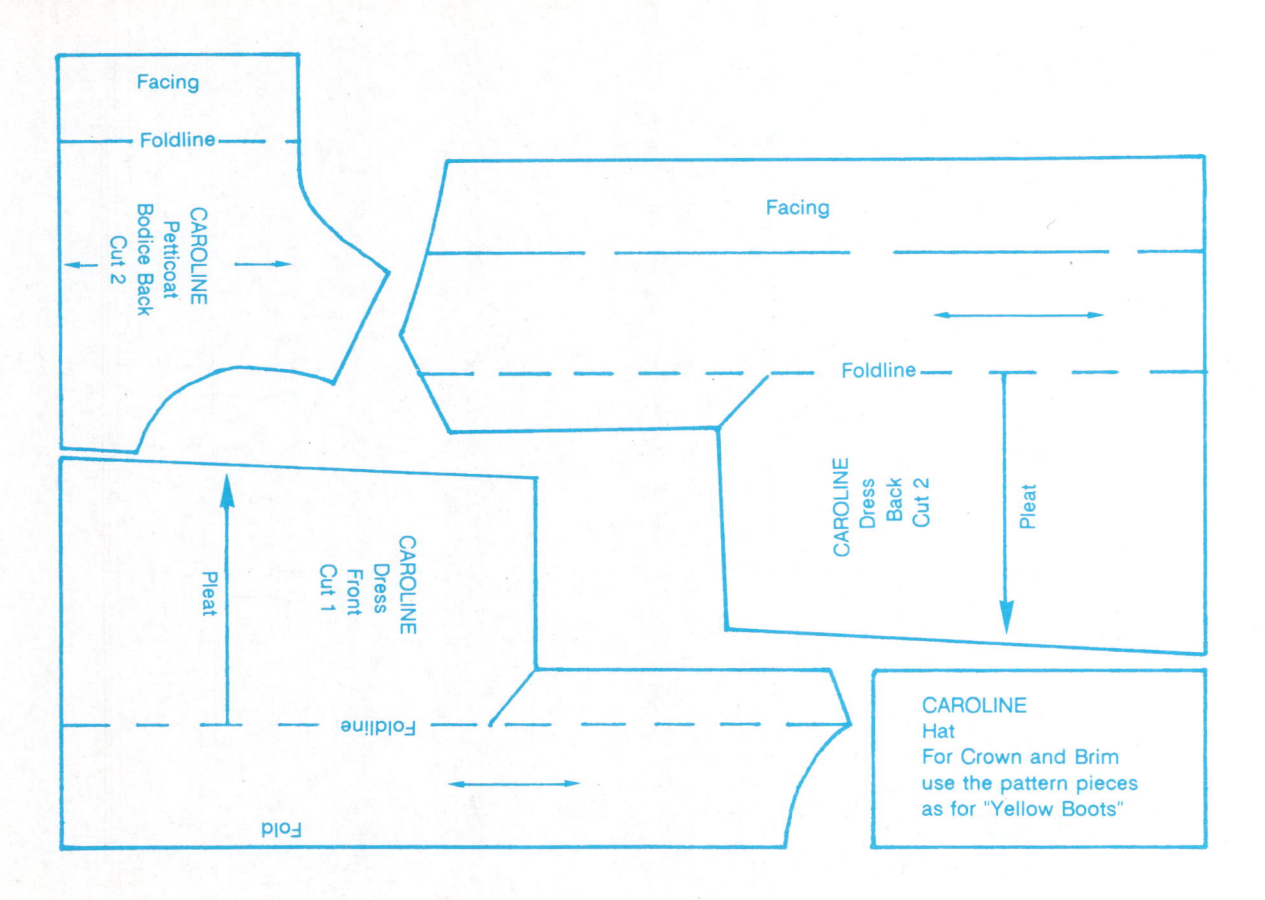

CAROLINE

Facing
Foldline
CAROLINE Petticoat Bodice Back Cut 2

Facing
Foldline
CAROLINE Dress Back Cut 2
Pleat

Pleat
CAROLINE Dress Front Cut 1
Foldline
Fold

CAROLINE
Hat
For Crown and Brim
use the pattern pieces
as for "Yellow Boots"

CAROLINE

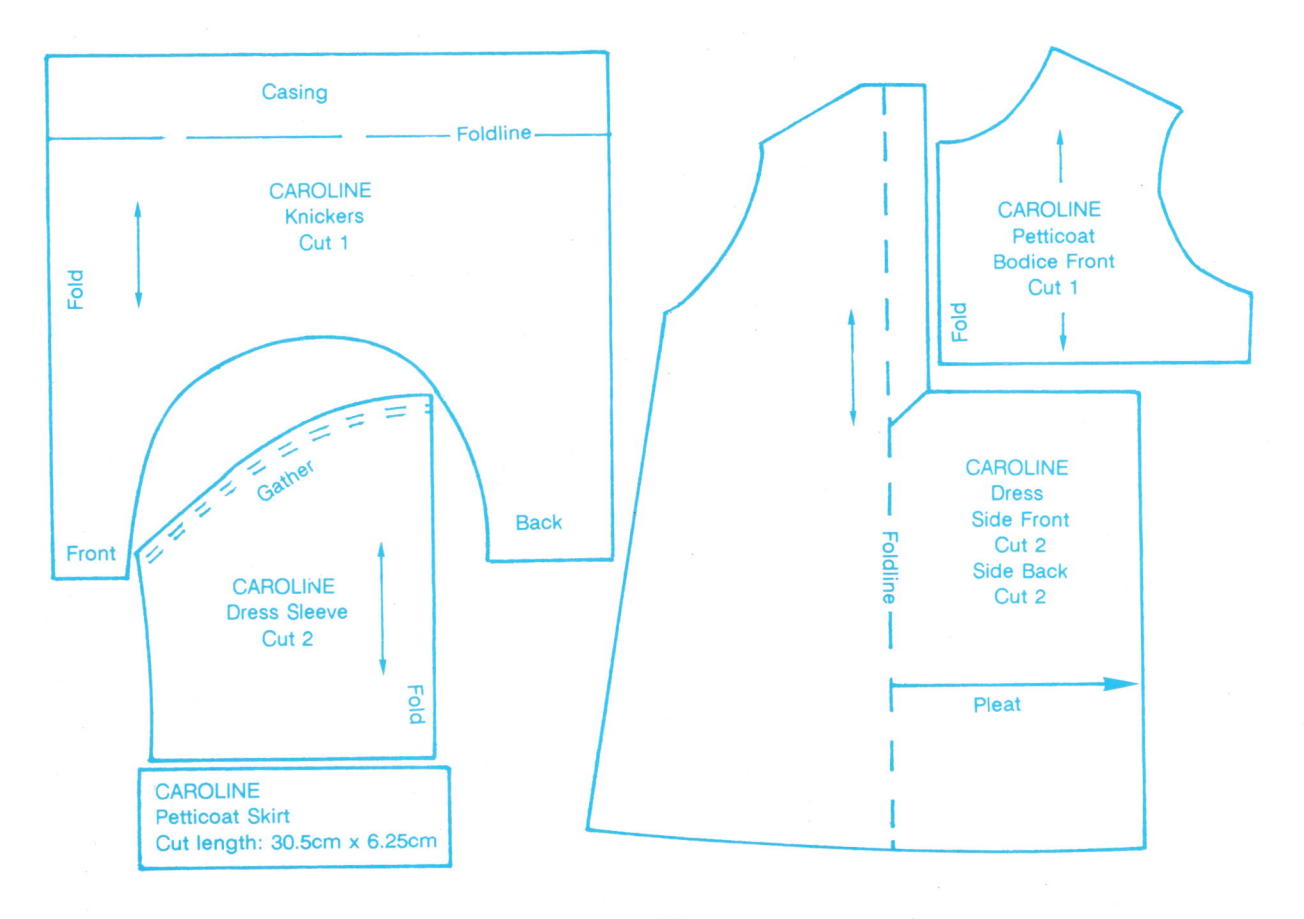

Casing

Foldline

CAROLINE
Knickers
Cut 1

Fold

Front

Gather

Back

CAROLINE
Dress Sleeve
Cut 2

Fold

CAROLINE
Petticoat Skirt
Cut length: 30.5cm x 6.25cm

CAROLINE
Petticoat
Bodice Front
Cut 1

Fold

CAROLINE
Dress
Side Front
Cut 2
Side Back
Cut 2

Foldline

Pleat

SWEET WILLIAM

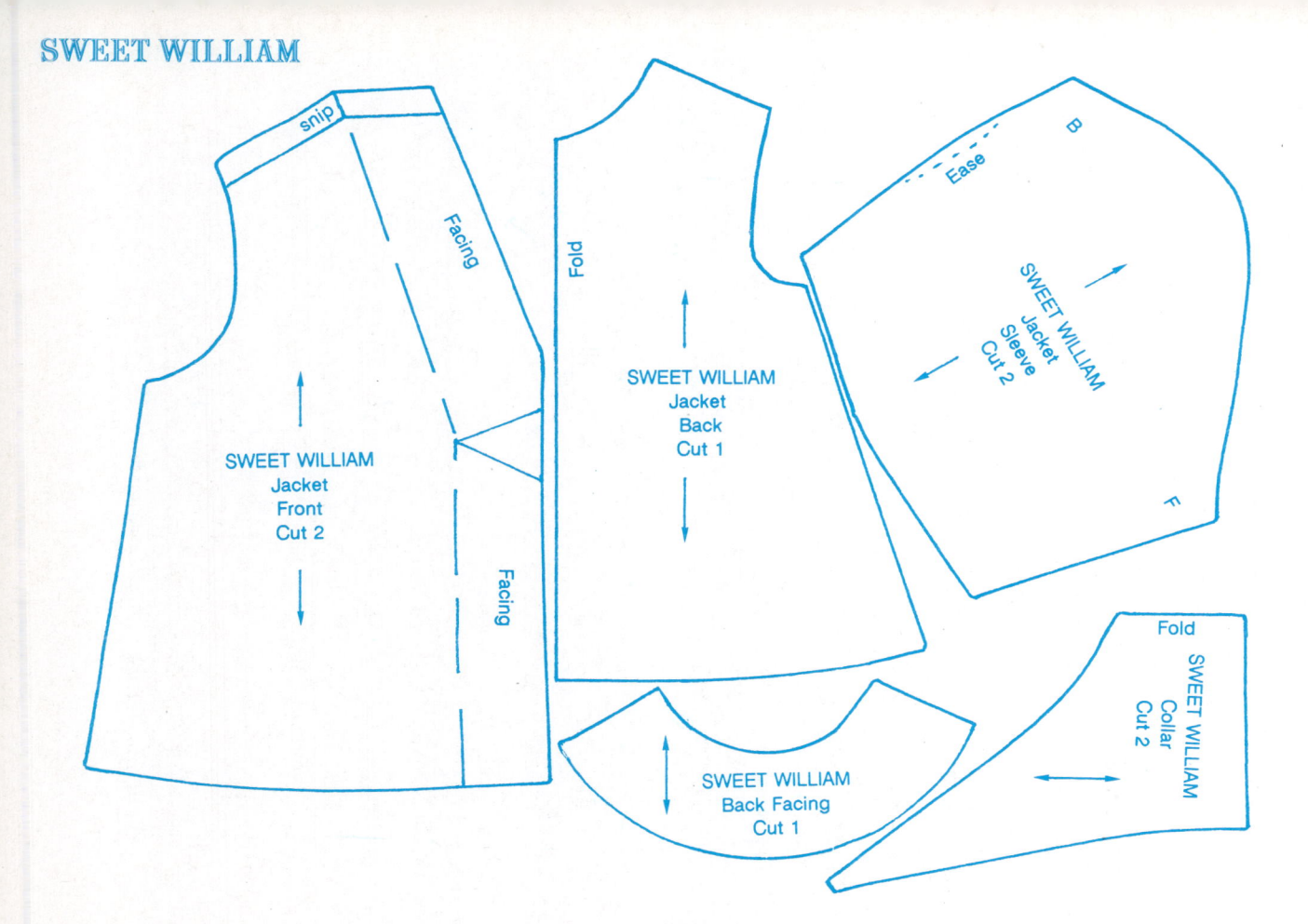

snip

Facing

SWEET WILLIAM
Jacket
Front
Cut 2

Facing

Fold

SWEET WILLIAM
Jacket
Back
Cut 1

Ease

B

SWEET WILLIAM
Jacket
Sleeve
Cut 2

F

SWEET WILLIAM
Back Facing
Cut 1

Fold

SWEET WILLIAM
Collar
Cut 2

40

SWEET WILLIAM

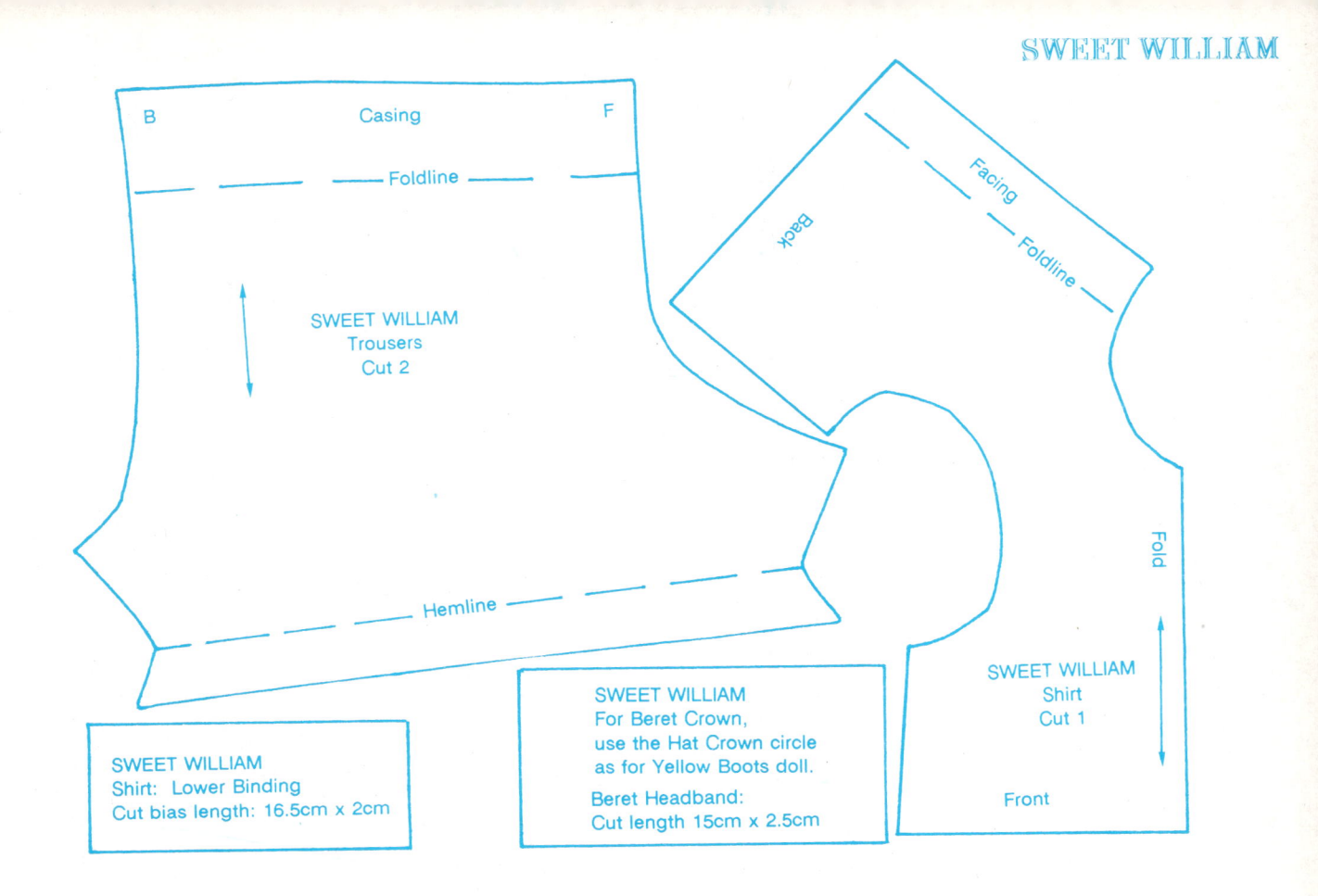

B Casing F
— Foldline —

SWEET WILLIAM
Trousers
Cut 2

Hemline

Back

Facing
— Foldline —

Fold

SWEET WILLIAM
Shirt
Cut 1

Front

SWEET WILLIAM
Shirt: Lower Binding
Cut bias length: 16.5cm x 2cm

SWEET WILLIAM
For Beret Crown,
use the Hat Crown circle
as for Yellow Boots doll.

Beret Headband:
Cut length 15cm x 2.5cm

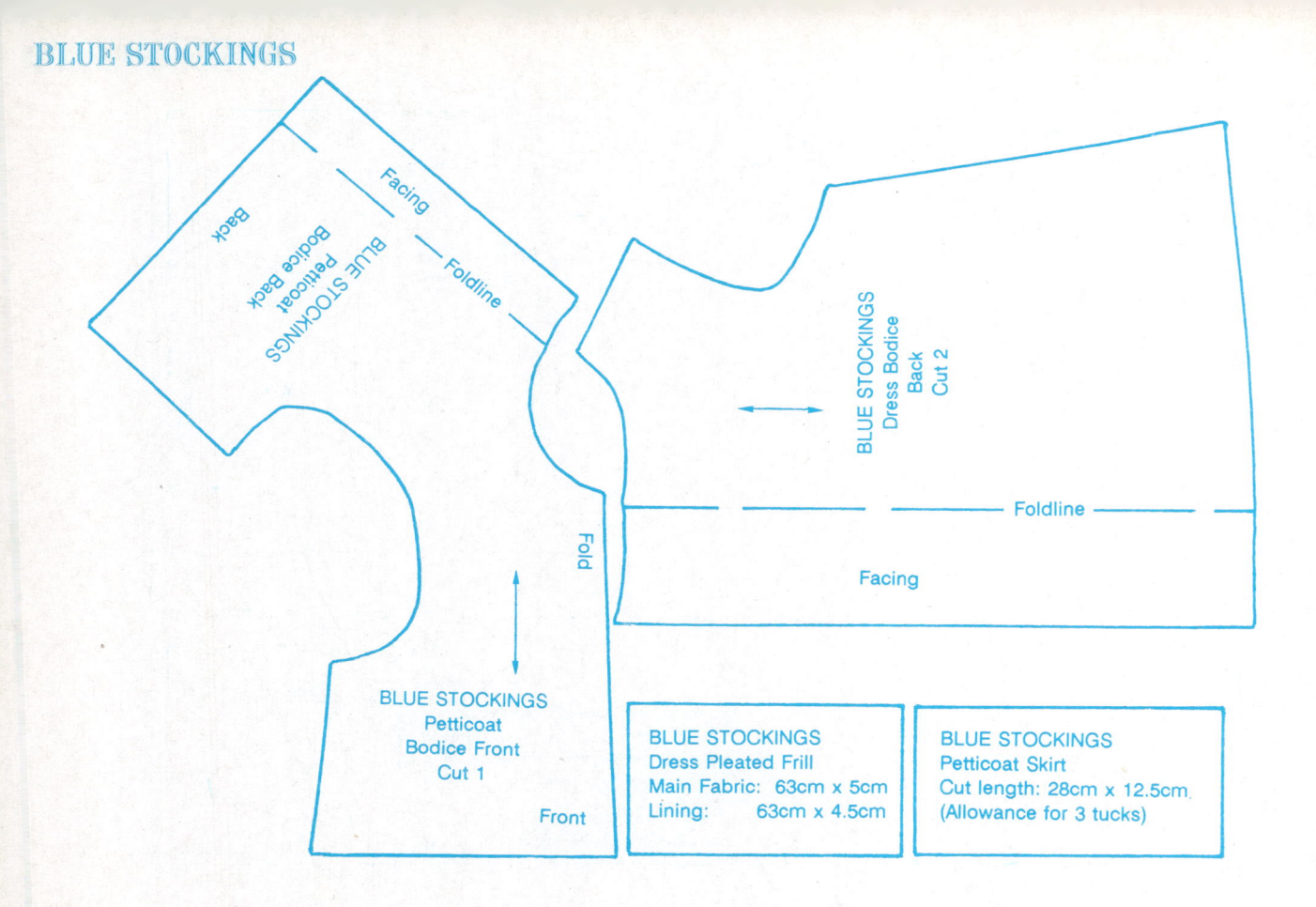

BLUE STOCKINGS

(Pattern pieces shown:)

- **BLUE STOCKINGS** Petticoat Bodice Back — Facing, Foldline, Back
- **BLUE STOCKINGS** Dress Bodice Back — Cut 2, Foldline, Facing
- **BLUE STOCKINGS** Petticoat Bodice Front — Cut 1, Fold, Front

BLUE STOCKINGS
Dress Pleated Frill
Main Fabric: 63cm x 5cm
Lining: 63cm x 4.5cm

BLUE STOCKINGS
Petticoat Skirt
Cut length: 28cm x 12.5cm
(Allowance for 3 tucks)

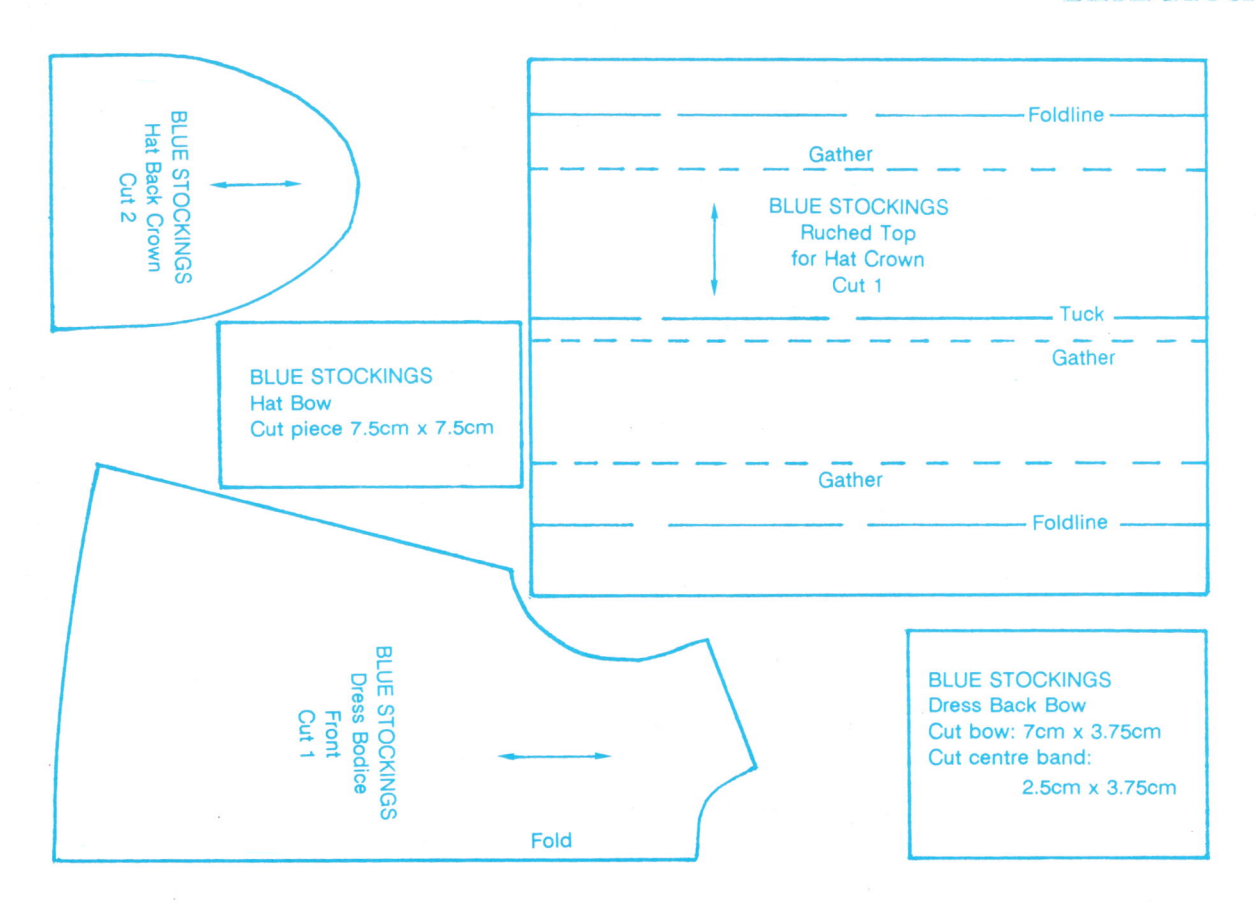

BLUE STOCKINGS

BLUE STOCKINGS
Hat Back Crown
Cut 2

Foldline
Gather

BLUE STOCKINGS
Ruched Top
for Hat Crown
Cut 1

Tuck
Gather

BLUE STOCKINGS
Hat Bow
Cut piece 7.5cm x 7.5cm

Gather
Foldline

BLUE STOCKINGS
Dress Bodice
Front
Cut 1

Fold

BLUE STOCKINGS
Dress Back Bow
Cut bow: 7cm x 3.75cm
Cut centre band:
    2.5cm x 3.75cm

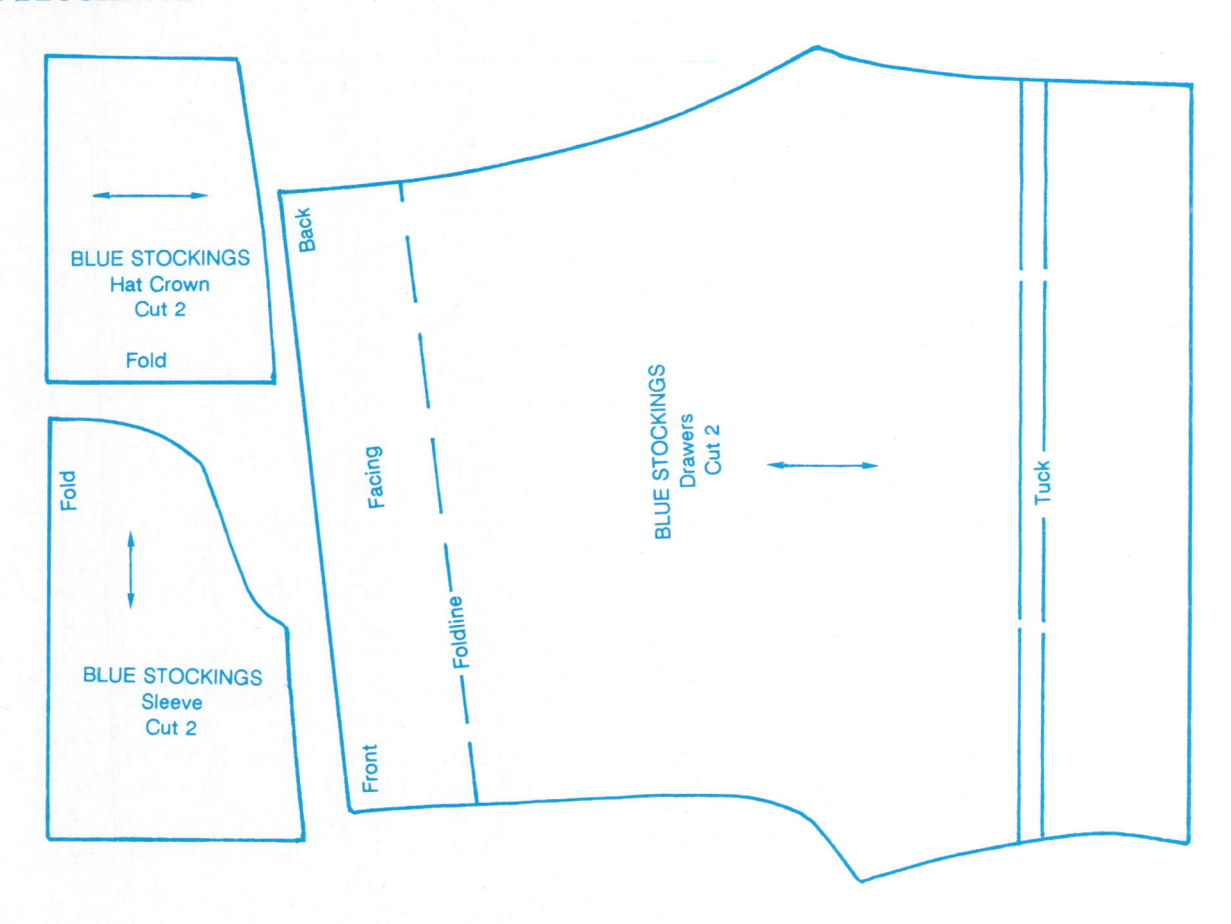

BLUE STOCKINGS

BLUE STOCKINGS
Hat Crown
Cut 2

Fold

Fold

BLUE STOCKINGS
Sleeve
Cut 2

Back

Facing

Foldline

Front

BLUE STOCKINGS
Drawers
Cut 2

Tuck

YELLOW BOOTS

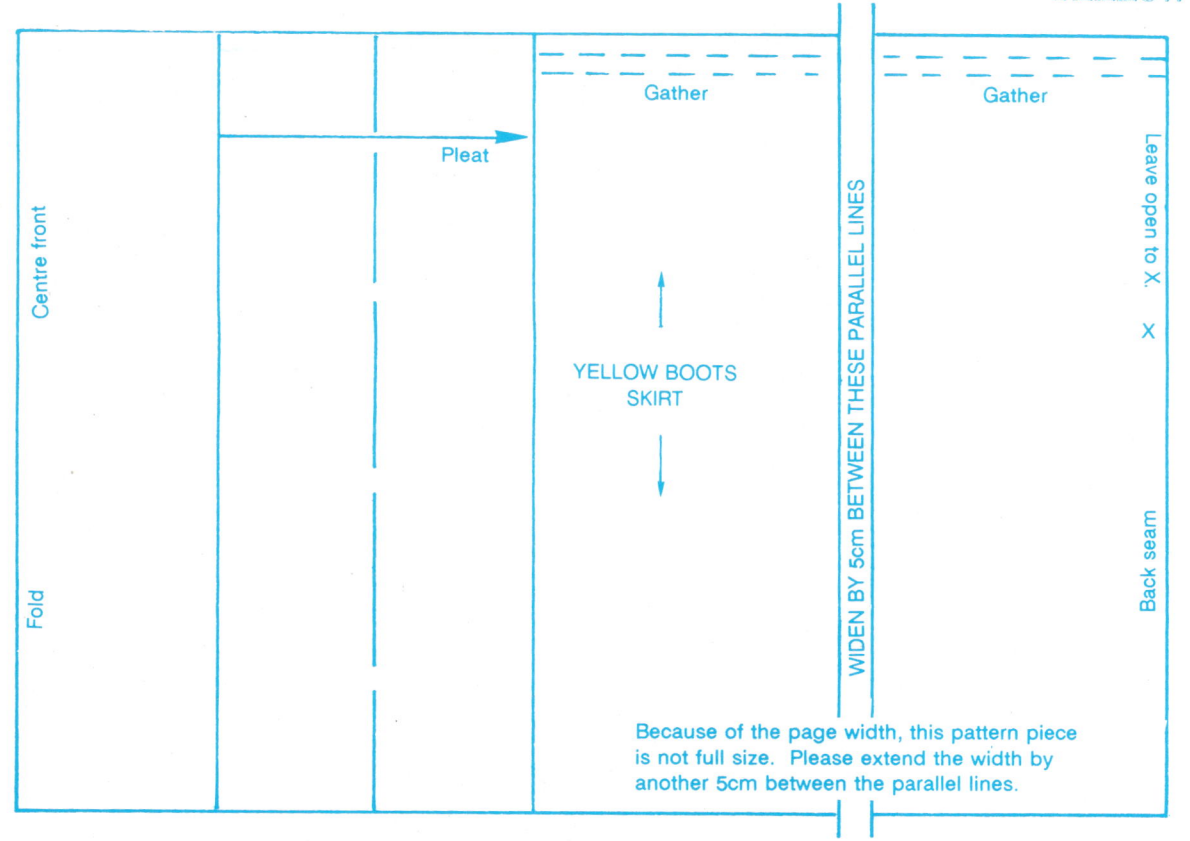

Gather — Gather

Pleat →

Centre front

Fold

Leave open to X.   X

Back seam

WIDEN BY 5cm BETWEEN THESE PARALLEL LINES

YELLOW BOOTS
SKIRT

Because of the page width, this pattern piece is not full size. Please extend the width by another 5cm between the parallel lines.

45

YELLOW BOOTS

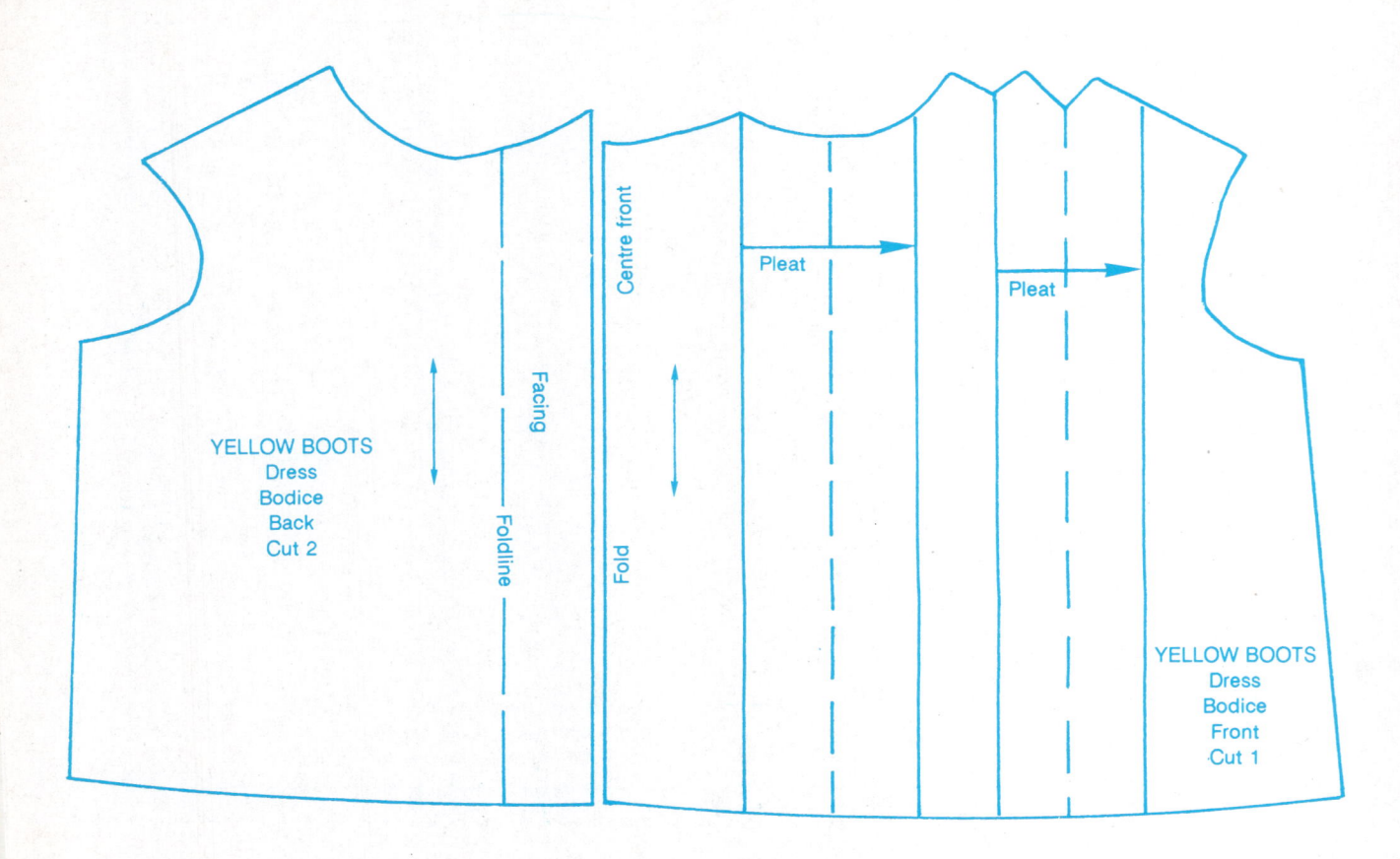

YELLOW BOOTS
Dress
Bodice
Back
Cut 2

Facing
Foldline

Centre front
Fold

Pleat
Pleat

YELLOW BOOTS
Dress
Bodice
Front
Cut 1

YELLOW BOOTS

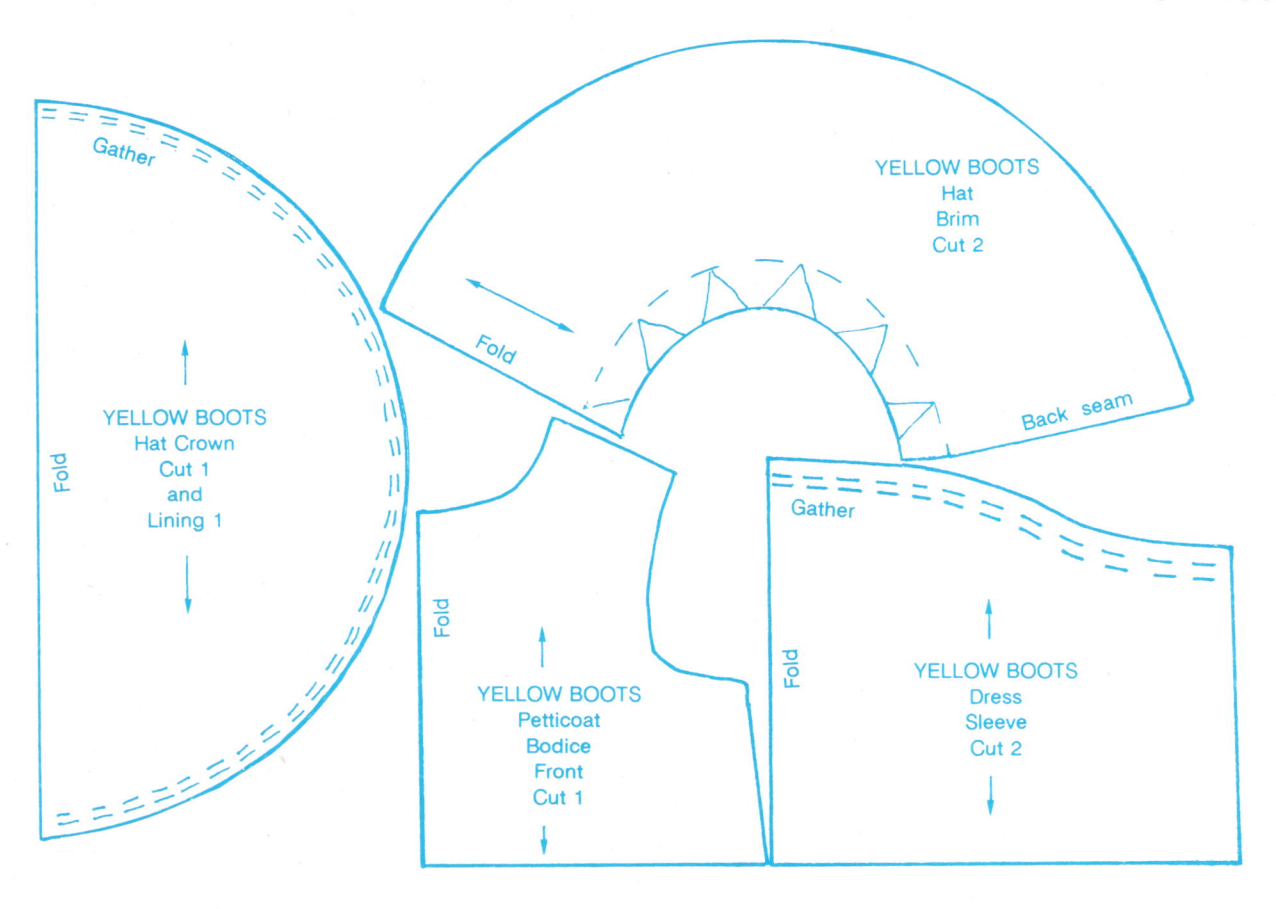

YELLOW BOOTS
Hat Brim
Cut 2

Gather

Fold

Back seam

YELLOW BOOTS
Hat Crown
Cut 1
and
Lining 1

Fold

YELLOW BOOTS
Petticoat
Bodice
Front
Cut 1

Fold

Gather

YELLOW BOOTS
Dress
Sleeve
Cut 2

Fold

YELLOW BOOTS

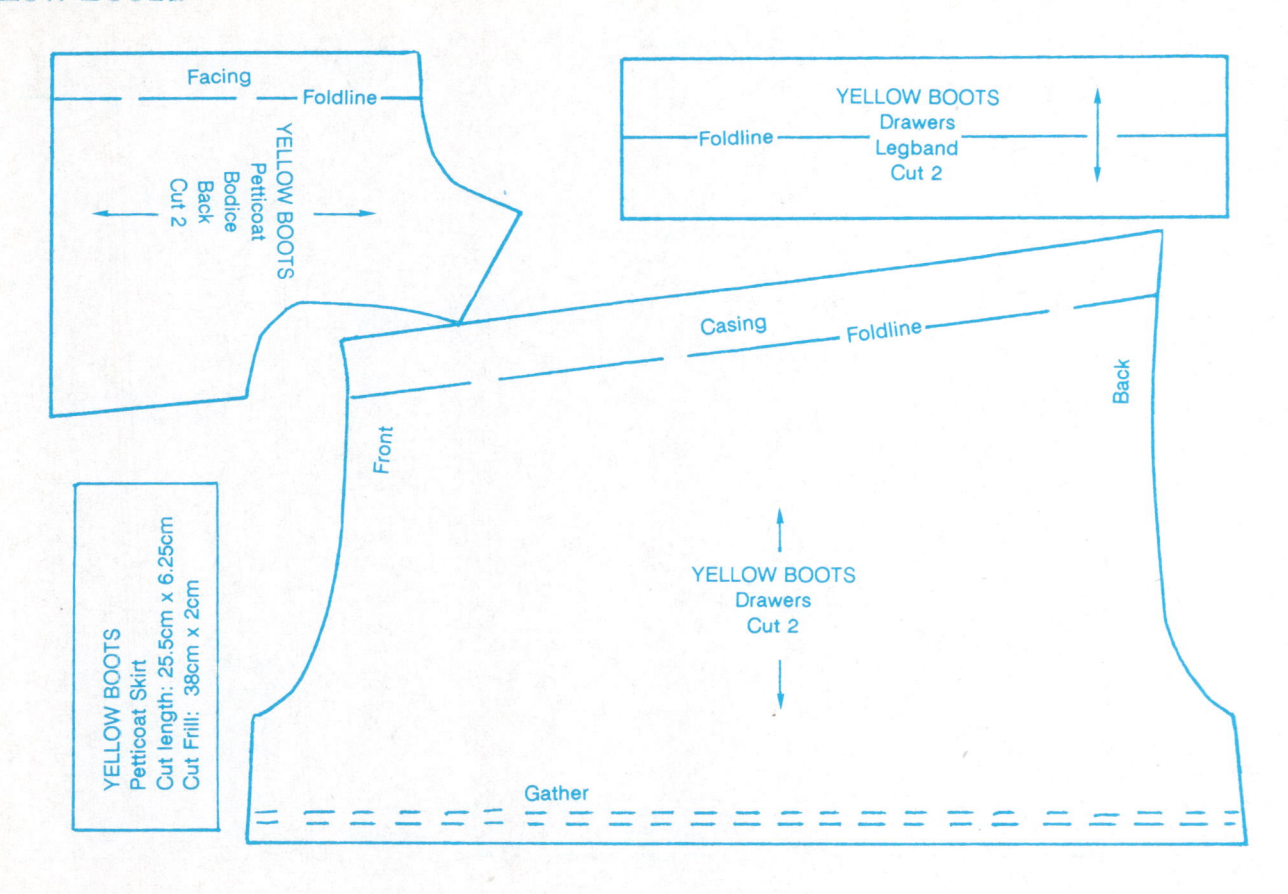

- Facing
- Foldline
- YELLOW BOOTS Petticoat Bodice Back Cut 2

- Foldline
- YELLOW BOOTS Drawers Legband Cut 2

- Casing
- Foldline
- Front
- Back
- YELLOW BOOTS Drawers Cut 2
- Gather

YELLOW BOOTS
Petticoat Skirt
Cut length: 25.5cm x 6.25cm
Cut Frill: 38cm x 2cm

48

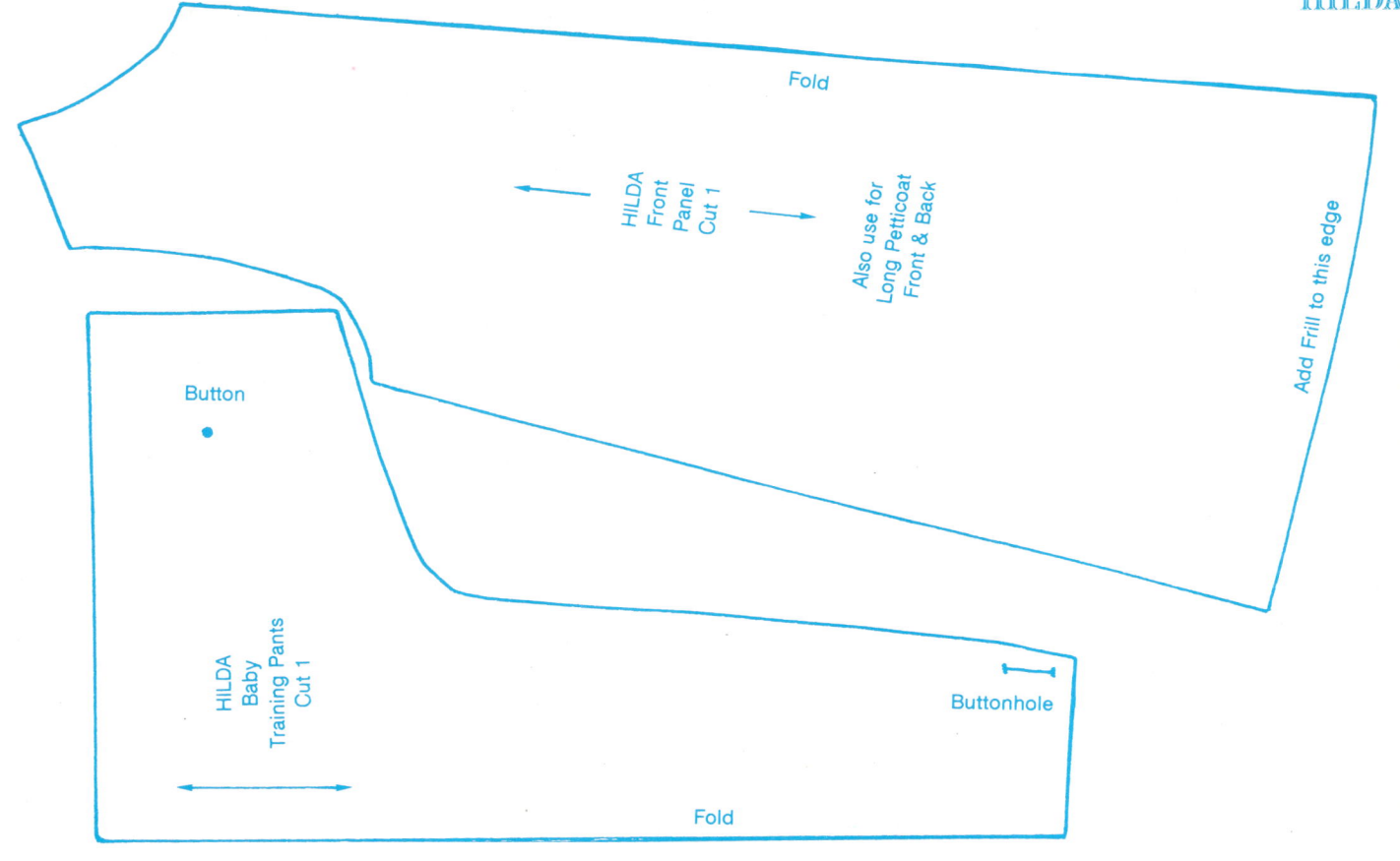

HILDA

Fold

← HILDA Front Panel Cut 1 →

Also use for Long Petticoat Front & Back

Add Frill to this edge

Button

HILDA Baby Training Pants Cut 1

Buttonhole

Fold

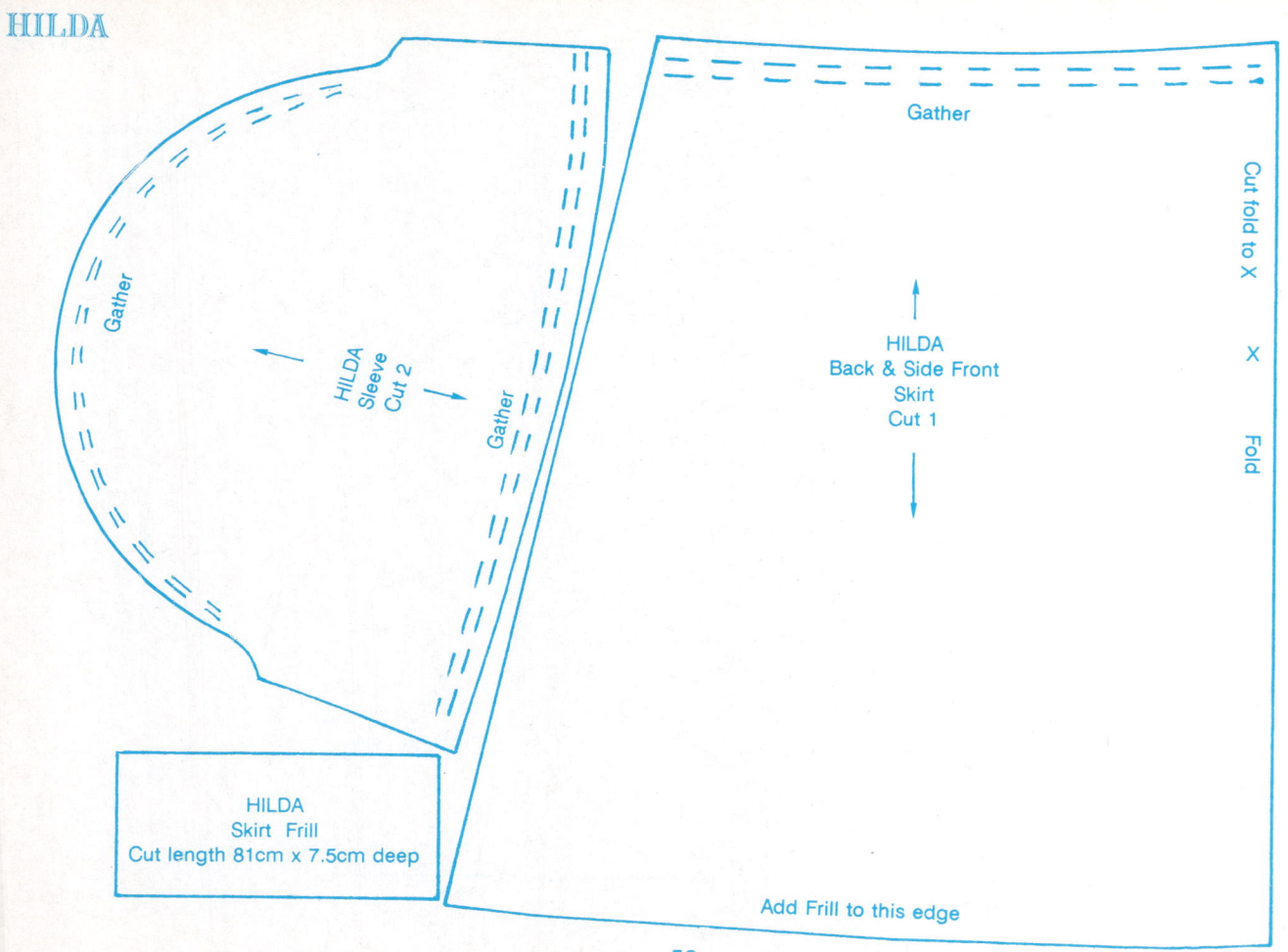

HILDA

Gather

Cut fold to X

X

Fold

Gather

HILDA
Sleeve
Cut 2

Gather

HILDA
Back & Side Front
Skirt
Cut 1

HILDA
Skirt Frill
Cut length 81cm x 7.5cm deep

Add Frill to this edge

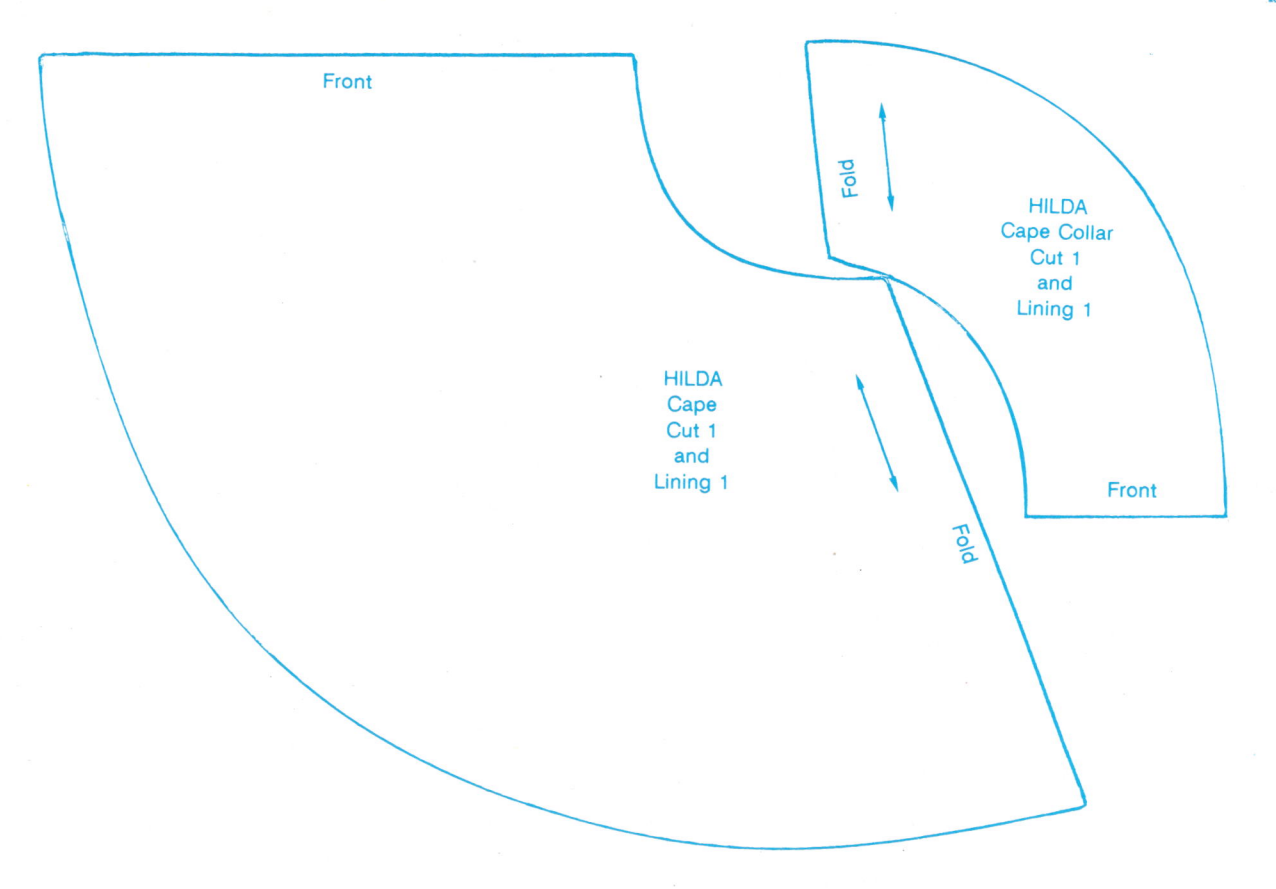

HILDA

Front

Fold

HILDA
Cape Collar
Cut 1
and
Lining 1

HILDA
Cape
Cut 1
and
Lining 1

Fold

Front

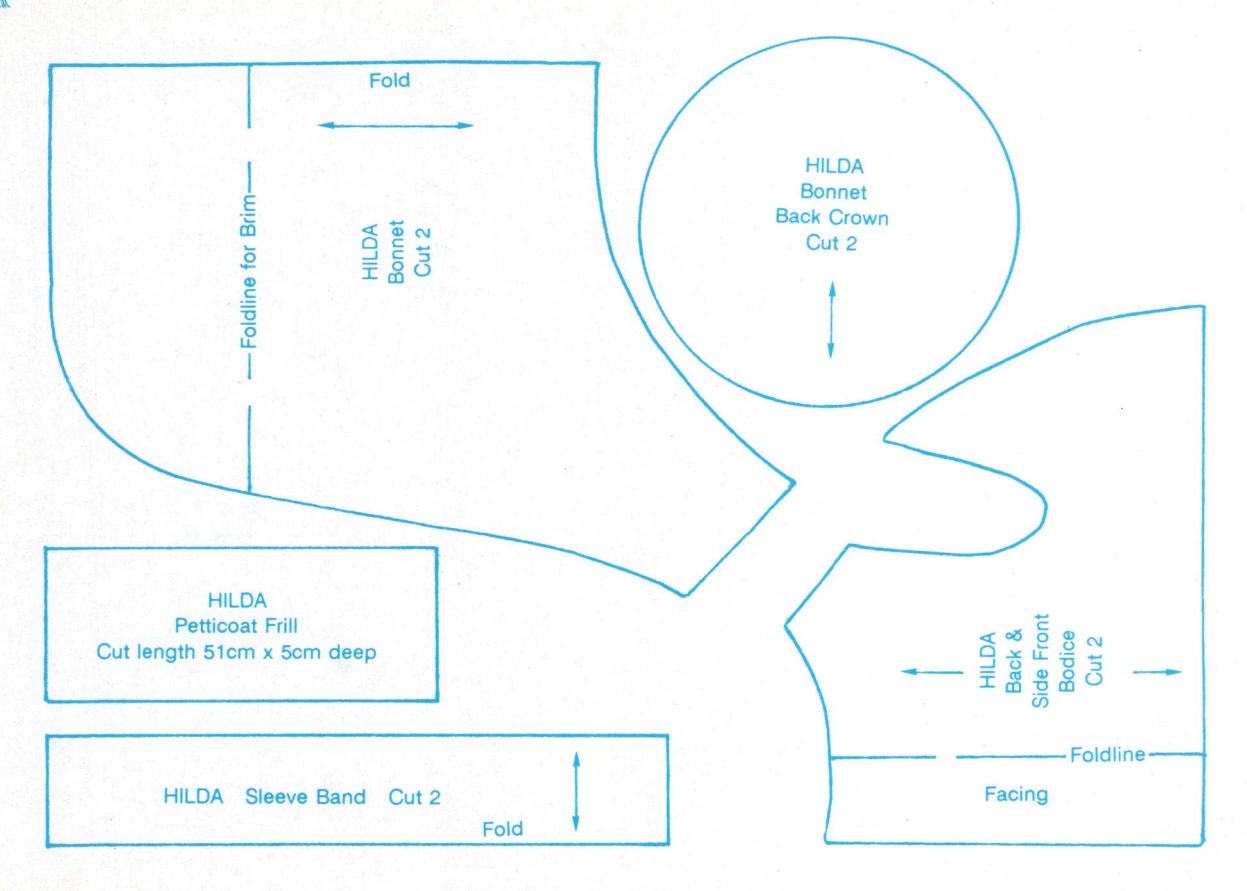

HILDA

HILDA Bonnet Cut 2
Foldline for Brim
Fold

HILDA Bonnet Back Crown Cut 2

HILDA Petticoat Frill
Cut length 51cm x 5cm deep

HILDA Sleeve Band Cut 2
Fold

HILDA Back & Side Front Bodice Cut 2
Foldline
Facing